TOPICS IN APPLIED GEOGRAPHY

THE GEOGRAPHY OF
URBAN CRIME

TOPICS IN APPLIED GEOGRAPHY
edited by Donald Davidson and John Dawson

David T. Herbert
University College of Swansea

THE GEOGRAPHY OF
URBAN CRIME

Longman
London
and New York

This book is dedicated to my brothers – LESLIE and TREVOR – with memories of our Rhondda days

Longman Group Limited
Longman House
Burnt Mill, Harlow, Essex, UK

*Published in the United States of America
by Longman Inc. New York*

First published 1982

British Library Cataloguing in Publication Data

Herbert, David, *1935–*
    The geography of urban crime. – (Topics in applied geography).
    1. Crime and criminals
    2. Cities and towns
    I Title   II. Series
    364'.91732   HV6030   80–41890

    ISBN 0-582-30046-0

Printed in Singapore by the Singapore National Printers (Pte) Ltd.

CONTENTS

LIST OF FIGURES

LIST OF TABLES

PREFACE

It is a feature of modern academic disciplines that their development has become typified by a proliferation of subdivisions. The significance of this trend can be alternatively viewed. For some it serves as a confirmation of the arbitrary nature of disciplinary boundaries, 'invented' as much for administrative as for intellectual purposes. The need for subdivisions is viewed as evidence of the inability of the disciplinary 'package' to contain its evolution and of the imperative to identify less rigid perspectives within a unified social science. For others the trend stands as a healthy response to a growth in their discipline which displays a willingness to develop along new paths. These trends have been discussed elsewhere (Herbert and Johnston, 1978) and it has been noted that although many new directions of study have emerged, they have rarely produced any severance from mainstream geography. A *branching* model was proposed in which new kinds of topical fields are accommodated but strong links with the central core of the discipline are maintained. Such a model admittedly uses the administrative convenience of an existing disciplinary framework but recognizes a methodological unity within each discipline which provides an academic *raison d'être*. Boundaries and compartments can be recognized but they are certainly not 'strait-jackets'; a good deal of recent research by geographers has consciously sought to avoid spatial fetishism and a model has been proposed (Herbert, 1979a) and is elaborated here which seeks to accommodate this eclecticism and its varying bonds with the core of the discipline.

The geography of crime is viewed in this context. Whereas the phenomenon studied gives the topical field its adjectival distinctiveness within geography, the methodologies and concepts used are grounded in the more general basis of the discipline. It is also argued that other social problems can be studied in very similar ways and that specific methodologies developed to study offences and offenders have general applicability. For this text, however, the central thrust is to demonstrate how a topic such as crime can be studied by geographers. It acknowledges the limitations of a purely *spatial* form of analysis and explores ways in which geographical research can widen its horizons and reorder its priorities. Whereas much research by geographers on crime, and indeed on other topics, has been heavily focused on the 'local interface' where environment in its various forms contains the outcomes of social processes, there is an increasing awareness of the need to examine the processes themselves and other levels of analysis. A trichotomy of levels concerned with the production, distribution and consumption of space is suggested in which research at all levels can be justified but the present record shows neglect of the first two.

Crime is a problem which can be readily identified and acknowledged by most people. There are issues of how it is defined and of who labels offences and offenders which need close attention, but whatever codification system is adopted it will not achieve complete consensus. If society has rules, someone has to invent them. The objective is to ensure that basic principles of equity and democracy are met both in the making of the rules and their enforcement. However crime and criminals are defined they represent a source of fear to large numbers of people and detract from their quality of life and sense of well-being. That fear and its consequences tends to be particularly concentrated in cities and in specific areas of cities where it forms one element of a more general problem. The 'facts' of crime, the way in which justice and policing are administered, the offenders and their victims form elements of a topical field towards which a geographical perspective is developing. There are academic insights to be offered and, more particularly in the context of this series, there is a practical application of research findings to be demonstrated. For the many hundreds of thousands of occupants of generally disadvantaged parts of cities in particular, crime is another factor which adds stress and distraction to their daily lives; if geographical research can offer some input to policies designed to help, it must be vigorously pursued.

Several circumstances combined to allow me a relatively clear period of time in which to write this book. I am firstly grateful to University College of Swansea for two terms sabbatical leave during 1980 which allowed me to concentrate on the actual process of writing. Invitations to visit American universities over a six-month period in the latter half of 1979 gave me access to ideas and information on the geography of crime in the United States. At the University of Oklahoma in particular I was able to discuss some of the issues in constructive ways and obtain criminal statistics for Oklahoma City. I am grateful to Police Chief Tom Heggy and his very efficient data analysis unit for the information relating to Oklahoma City. Keith Harries at Oklahoma State University was a source of many contacts and valued discussions over this period. Similarly, at Norman, Jim Bohland and Chris Smith helped in various ways and Bill Turner had the patience and interest to sit through my 'crime lecture' on three different occasions and made some insightful observations. For the South Wales data I express my gratitude to the Chief Constable of the South Wales Constabulary. Guy Lewis provided the cartographic skills necessary for the presentation of some of the data and is, as always, much appreciated; Mary Owens typed the manuscript with great efficiency and put me right on a few points. Lastly, my personal thanks to my wife, Tonwen, for her help and support; to my mother-in-law, Mrs M.J. Maddock, for hers; and to my children, Aled and Nia, who provided no more than their usual level of distraction.

David T. Herbert
University College of Swansea
September 1980

ACKNOWLEDGEMENTS

We are grateful to the following for permission to reproduce copyright material: Association of American Geographers for Figs. 3.2, 3.3, 3.4 and 3.5 from an article by K. D. Harries in the *Proceedings A.A.G.* **5**, 1973 pp. 97–101: Ballinger Publishing Company for Tables 3.1, 3.2, 3.3, 3.4, 3.7 and 3.8 from *Residential Crime* by T. A. Repetto, Copyright 1974: B. T. Batsford Limited for a map on page 132 of *Crime and the Industrial Society in the 19th Century* by J. T. Tobias 1967: Jonathan Cape Limited for map 2 page 66 from *Juvenile Delinquency* by J. H. Bagot 1971: The Controller of Her Majesty's Stationery Office for Fig. 1.1 p. 4 from *Tackling Vandalism* ed. by R. V. G. Clarke 1978 published by the Home Office Research Unit (Study number 47); The Institute of British Geographers for Fig. 2 pp. 478/9 and Tables I and II pp. 481–2 from 'The Study of Delinquency Areas: A Social Geographical Approach', *Transactions, Institute of British Geographers*, N. S. **1**, 472–92: McGraw-Hill Book Company for Figs. 3.5 and 5.7 from *The Geography of Crime and Justice* by K. D. Harries 1974: Macmillan Publishing Co. Inc. (and The Architectural Press Limited) for Fig. 21 p. 40 and Tables 4 p. 46: 10 and 11 p. 85: 1 p. 28 from *Defensible Space* Copyright © 1972 by Oscar Newman: Oklahoma State University for Fig. 19 p. 79 and Fig. 25 p. 86 from *Burglary: An Ecological and Aerial-Photographic Analysis* – an unpublished M.Sc. thesis by J. A. Sturdevant 1979 and Fig. 5 p. 115 and the University of Oklahoma for Fig. 7 p. 117 from *The Criminal's Image of the City* an unpublished Ph.D thesis by R. L. Carter 1974: Oxford University Press for Fig. 7.3 p. 33 from *Social Problems and the City: Geographical Perspectives* ed. by D. T. Herbert and D. M Smith 1979: Praeger Publishers Copyright © 1978 map 2.8 p. 29 map 6.3 p. 96 from *The Geography of Law and Justice* by K. D. Harries and S. D. Brunn: Tavistock Publications Limited for map 3 p. 75 from *The Urban Criminal* by J. Baldwin and A. E. Bottoms 1975: *Tijdchrift voor Economische – Sociale Geografie* for Fig. 3 p. 90 and Tables 5.1, 5.2, 5.3, 5.4 and 5.5 from 'An Areal and Ecological Analysis of Delinquency Residence in Cardiff 1961 and 1971' by D. T. Herbert 1977, **68**, 83–99: The University of Chicago Press for map 8 p. 54 Fig. 1A p. 69 and map 73 p. 359 from *Juvenile Delinquency and Urban Areas* by C. R. Shaw and H. D. McKay 1942, 1969 and 1972.

CHAPTER 1
DATA BASES AND REGIONAL PATTERNS

INTRODUCTION

The notion of a 'geography' of urban crime can in some ways be viewed as yet another attempt to compartmentalize the study of one of society's more apparent problems into the bounds of a conventional discipline. To some extent it is acknowledged that an objective of this book is to explore ways in which a range of geographical perspectives, or the practices and methodologies developed by geographers over the past few decades, can add a dimension, hitherto largely neglected, to the broad field of criminology. It can also be readily acknowledged, however, that geographical perspectives have no speical claims in relation to problem-solving but rather offer a limited and partial role which must ultimately be fused with the limited and partial roles offered by other disciplines in the attempt to understand the phenomena being investigated. The broader objective therefore is to identify the context into which a geography of urban crime must fit; a context which is both multidisciplinary and contains a range of 'levels' of analysis. Criminology, a field of study with an existence covering two centuries, has attracted a plurality of disciplines. Geography, which has figured very little in this plurality is now worthy of more explicit attention. The fact that this geographical perspective is being explored at a time when in criminology, and indeed within the social sciences at large, disciplinary boundaries are becoming blurred and less relevant provides a qualifying context for any attempt to advocate its special merits. The arguments for a unified social science, with greater emphasis on the interfaces between disciplines rather than upon their traditional cores, are in fact found within human geography (Herbert, 1980b).

The existence of social problems may be in the eye of the beholder, and attempts to identify problems *per se* may divert attention from the holistic nature of society (Lee, 1979), but there can be little doubt that crime constitutes a major perceived problem for the urban dwellers of Western societies. Major national surveys in the United States (NCJISS, 1977) show that significant numbers of people live in fear of victimization; fears which are particularly widespread among sub-groups, such as the elderly, and in some areas, such as the inner cities. Whatever the justification for researching the origins of problems and the fundamental issue of *social reproduction* (Lee, 1979), there is a crime problem currently experienced by large numbers of people in urban environments which is a research priority. The official statistics of crime, which undoubtedly understate the problem, tell us with remarkable consistency that rates of crime and delinquency are increasing and that cities are at the core of such increases. These trends and their spatial expressions can be traced but it is pertinent first to scrutinizé official statistics on crime in their own right. Whereas these form the basic data source for much research, there have been severe doubts expressed regarding their reliability and representativeness. In this chapter therefore the nature of official statistics on crime and delinquency will be discussed prior to their use in an attempt to portray broad patterns of crime in the United Kingdom and the United States.

SOURCES OF CRIME DATA

At an aggregate scale there is a considerable supply of statistical data relating to crime and delinquency in most Western societies. In the United Kingdom, the Home Office publishes its detailed *Criminal Statistics* on an annual basis and, within the limits of the aggregations used, these show variations in offence rates over time, comparisons between types of offences, and interregional differences. In addition to information on offences by police districts, the *Criminal Statistics* contain data on sentencing patterns at the various levels of courts, both crown and magistrates' courts, by police district and crown court centre. Information on applications for legal aid are provided for petty sessional divisions. This last category of information is composed of the largest number of territorial units but for the largest sets of data the police districts, of which there are only forty-three in England and Wales, form the standard geographical framework. For the United States, the annual *Uniform Crime Reports* contain both a large amount of data and a considerable range of analyses, and comparable publications exist in other countries of the developed world. Although form and content have changed over time, long historical runs of such data allow temporal analyses to be made. Mayhew (1862) used police district data for his mid-nineteenth-century surveys of crime and delinquency by counties in England and Wales; the 'cartographic school' (Phillips, 1972) flourished between 1830 and 1880 depicting regional variations in crime rates within European countries.

Over time there have been technical changes in the presentation of data which make comparative analysis more difficult. Some of these involve definitions of offences and changing forms of punishment; others, more directly relevant to spatial analyses, involve adjustments to boundaries of police force areas which form the basic data recording units. In the mid-1960s, for example, there were major reappraisals, affecting both the general form and content of the *Criminal Statistics*, accompanying an amalgamation of police forces in England and Wales from the previous 125 to 43. Besides reducing the amount of detail possible in terms of geographical variation, these new police force areas maintain the lack of correspondence with other administrative districts which has been a consistent feature of the data source. Central to this unique set of areas is its mismatch with areas for which census data are published; calculation of population bases becomes a time-consuming procedure, often with a strong estimation ingredient. Even the eight regions covered by the regional conferences of the Association of Chief Police Officers do not correspond with the nine standard regions used for regional statistics in other Government publications covering England and Wales. In these respects the American *Uniform Crime Reports* have the advantage that their area bases, of States, standard metropolitan areas and cities with over 25 000 inhabitants, are easily related to population bases from census data without recourse to special tabulations.

A further technical point in the use of criminal statistics concerns the definitions of offences which are used. The general distinction between indictable and non-indictable offences is usually made in terms of procedures used to deal with offenders (McClintock and Avison, 1968). Subsequent changes in police and judicial practice have reduced the effectiveness of indictability as an indicator of serious offences. Place of trial is no longer an effective index as no less than 90 per cent of persons proceeded against in respect of indictable offences are in fact dealt with summarily, while over 10 per cent of those processed through higher courts were charged with non-indictable offences.

Given this erosion of the accuracy of the traditional division of more serious from less serious offences, various researchers and official agencies have adopted their own indicators. Best known of these is perhaps the FBI Index Crime measure which is used in the annual *Uniform Crime Reports*. Here the most serious offences are listed as criminal homicide, forcible rape, robbery, aggravated assault, burglary, larceny over a stated value and auto-theft. McClintock and Avison (1968) used a set of Class I crimes which they described as primarily consisting of major indictable offences which are normally tried in a higher court before judge and jury. They also monitored trends in 'selected major crimes' composed of murder, attempt to murder, felonious wounding, rape, robbery, breaking and entering, and larceny (the latter two categorized in terms of loss values). Composite indices of this kind illustrate the more general problem of classifying very large numbers of offences into manageable categories. Harries (1974) suggested that there were over 2800 Federal crimes in the United States and a larger number at State and local levels. The *Uniform Crime Reports* divide offences into twenty-nine main categories and the *Criminal Statistics* for England and Wales use around seventy main classes of indictable offences, some of which contain up to twenty subdivisions. Geographers in the United States (Harries, 1974; Pyle *et al.*, 1974) have tended to rely largely on the seven FBI Index crime rates. Clearly rationalizations of this kind can be justified in order to make sense of an enormous and diffuse body of data and also to obtain best bases for comparative analyses. Official crime rates are normally calculated against base populations of 100 000 but offence-specific rates which use more relevant base populations (see Boggs, 1966) are more telling measures. These will be discussed below; it can also be noted that both absolute and relative incidence rates are important. Until 1958 American crime rates were calculated against previous census populations – leading to artificial decrease in census years – but in England and Wales annual estimates are used in intercensal years.

ISSUES ON THE USE OF OFFICIAL STATISTICS

Despite this apparent surfeit of statistical bases from which to develop analyses, few data sources are regarded with more scepticism and mistrust. Sources of dissatisfaction include collection and classification procedures, definitions, the nature of crime and the motivations of attempts to record it. This book will use official criminal statistics on several scales in order to depict patterns of *known* offences and *known* offenders as bases for discussion and analysis. It is first essential, however, to look at these official statistics in a critical way. This discussion can be structured under a number of headings: underrepresentation, representativeness, and misrepresentation.

Underrepresentation

All researchers recognize that official statistics do not represent the total crime picture. This 'underrepresentation' – the fact that only a fraction of all offences and offenders enter official records – arises from several sources. First, as Table 1.1 shows, clear-up rates vary considerably by type of offence but are on average little above 40 per cent. Carr-Hill and Sterns (1979) calculated similar overall clear-up rates in England and Wales for 1961, 1966, and 1971. Given clear-up rates of this order, the first comment on underrepresentation is that only a minority of offenders are brought to justice and are thus known to the police. This highlights one distinction which will be used in later chapters, namely that between offences and offenders. The police know a great deal more about offences committed than they know about offenders; underrepresentation of the latter is therefore greater. Variability within type of offence should also be noted, violent offenders have a high probability of detection.

Table 1.1 Police clear-up rates by type of offence in England and Wales, 1969 and 1978

OFFENCE GROUP	1969	1978
Violence against person	81	77
Sexual offences	77	76
Burglary	34	32
Robbery	40	30
Theft and handling	40	40
Fraud and forgery	80	84
Criminal damage	38	30
Other indictable offences	91	92
Total (all offences)	42	42

Figures are percentages.
Source: Data extracted from *Criminal Statistics*, 1978, HMSO, London

Other sources of underrepresentation affect the number of offences recorded in official statistics. Some offences, for example, may be known to the police or other law-enforcing agencies but do not enter official records. An offence may be regarded as too trivial or lacking in substantive evidence or complaint; it may be dealt with summarily without recourse to any official recording procedure. This source of underrepresentation is likely to vary considerably over time and space with local policing procedures and rule interpretation. Harries (1974) suggests that in the United States police reporting may be affected by the level of professionalism of the police and by local political considerations. Carr-Hill and Sterns (1979) gathered evidence on variations in police reporting and on the amount of discretion they exercise; some significant points emerged. Firstly, the police make far more discretionary determinations in individual cases than virtually any other class of administrator. Secondly, the amount of discretion exercised tends to increase as one moves *down* the police hierarchy and is greatest at the first point of contact between police officer and offence or offender. Both these facts indicate the significance of the police in their roles as urban gatekeepers or managers whose discretionary decisions affect the crime rate. With the present state of knowledge on police reporting this use of discretionary power can neither be adequately generalized nor theorized, but its empirical effects are not doubted and, as it involves the non-recording of offences, it contributes to the underrepresentation of official statistics.

The 'dark area' constitutes both the best-known and the least understood source of underrepresentation in official criminal statistics. It broadly involves offences which occur but which are never known by the police. Firstly, there are offences which may go unnoticed, such as acts of vandalism on empty property, theft of a small number of items out of a large stock, or even potentially more serious issues such as the fate of missing persons. Secondly, there are offences which are noticed by the victim but are not reported to the police, such non-reporting may stem from a variety of reasons: fear of intimidation, desire to have no involvement with the police, or mere dismissal of the offence as trivial. Thirdly, there are offences which witnesses may observe or even become involved in but do not report. It is in this third category that underrepresentation is probably highest and the general issue involved, that of public cooperation with police, has become one of national concern. The extent of non-reporting will vary with the seriousness of the offence. Belson (1975) reported a range of reporting levels from 99 per cent willing to file a report if their house was burgled to 33 per cent if they knew someone was selling stolen property. Hawkins (1973) interviewed 1411 people in Seattle and found that 744 had been victims of at least one offence in the previous year, and of these 345 had been reported to the police but only 34 per cent of these reports came from the victims. There are clearly barriers to communication between the public, including victims, and the police which add significantly to the 'dark area' of unknown or unrecorded offences. The extent of non-communication will vary with type of offence and also with type of witness; some British immigrant communities, for example, may be less likely to report a range of offences at times when local relations between police/public are perceived to be poor.

These are sources of the 'dark area'. What is its size? Estimates vary with some general suggestion that only 15 to 25 per cent of all crimes committed in England and Wales are officially recorded (Hood and Sparks, 1970). Although American studies suggest non-reporting of serious delinquent offences, British research emphasizes the trivial character of much unrecorded crime. Although both surveillance and reporting procedures have recently been upgraded, shop-lifting has contained some striking examples of underrecording. Sellin (1937) calculated that of 5314 thefts known to three Philadelphia stores, 1423 led to arrests by store detectives and only 230 to actual prosecution. This dark area in police statistics of over 5000 offences is 96 per cent, without estimating the offences *not* known to the stores. More generally, two different strategies have been used to assess the extent of the dark area. Self-report studies, widely used among juveniles, involve the questioning of groups about illegal acts which they have committed, whether or not these have led to apprehension. Many of these studies suggest that the dark area is very large indeed. Elmhorn (1965) studied schoolboys in Stockholm and found that 57 per cent admitted to at least one offence; his estimate was that of the 1430 serious offences admitted, only in forty-one cases was the culprit known to the police. West and Farringdon (1973) discovered that 90 per cent of a sample of teenage boys admitted to relatively trivial offences, but only 7 to 12 per cent claimed to have been involved in serious offences. Carr-Hill and Sterns (1979), summarizing this evidence, suggested that the volume of events which could be classed as indictable crimes must be several times the recorded annual figure. Victimization surveys provide another means of estimating the dark area. Hood and Sparks (1970), from American evidence, suggested that twice as many major crimes were committed as were known to the police, and a methodologically sounder survey in Washington showed 38 per cent of a sample to have been victims of offences over a twelve-month period compared with a police estimate of 10 per cent.

Both self-report and victimization survey methods are open to doubt. There are problems of sample size, of time period over which accurate recall can be expected, and of the reliability of responses in general. Lack of consistency in replicative studies seems to underline these doubts. Overall, however, such studies do confirm a large dark area and the fact that official statistics considerably understate the level of crime.

Representativeness

A second problem with official statistics concerns the extent to which the 'sample' of offences and offenders which they offer is representative of the overall pattern. There is evidence that some types of offence are less likely to be reported to the police or recorded by the police than others. At both notification and processing stages, 'shrinkage' is likely to occur. In Washington (Hood and Sparks, 1970) police statistics accounted for less than half the offences which respondents claimed to have reported. Use of discretionary police powers was held to be the explanation for this but whether these are used in a consistent way is questionable. Again, the high levels of charges arising from occasional police purges on issues such as pornography, soft drugs, and drinking and driving, suggests that real levels of offences may be hidden by official attitudes towards them.

Discretionary decision-making may inadvertently lead to imbalances in the representativeness of data, more serious have been allegations of bias arising from official attitudes towards particular classes of offender. Many researchers (Mays, 1963) argue that official statistics may contain a bias towards working-class offenders in that the police are more likely to allow parental sanctions to replace legal sanctions in middle-class areas, and some guiding legislation may actually encourage such attitudes. Other studies (Russell, 1973) suggest that bias is practised against previous known offenders; the police develop 'stereotypes' and seek out suspects in relation to offences whether there is any direct evidence to link them to that specific offence or not. Russell's study of Brighton showed that over half the suspects checked were either previously known offenders or were classed as 'deviants'. An associated feature is that particular residential districts are policed more intensively and recorded offence and offender rates may be higher as a direct consequence:

> It appears that both the police and the public have definite stereotypes about the type of offence and offender which should be dealt with by criminal law; seriousness of offence is certainly a major criterion for official action, but so also are persistence in offending, lack of family support, membership of street corner group, and dress and demeanour that indicate a self image of toughness and anti-authoritarianism (Hood and Sparks, 1970, p. 78).

Bottomley and Coleman (1976) recognize the arguments on the selectivity of police law enforcement work but emphasize the sources of bias in public attitudes towards offences and offenders; police are reactive to public crime reporting, and much of the selectivity occurs before they become involved.

The net result of selective reporting and police discretion is a set of official statistics in which males vastly outnumber female offenders; low socio-economic groups, younger males, and some ethnic minorities are overrepresented. Despite these sources of disquiet, however, research aiming to show that 'hidden' delinquency is different in kind to 'official' delinquency is not conclusive. As the police do not proceed against all offenders, many hidden delinquents would not anyway enter official records. Gold (1966) suggests that whereas some bias against working-class youths is likely, official statistics do not seriously misrepresent their activities; similar conclusions are likely to emerge from the Sheffield crime suveys (Baldwin and Bottoms, 1976). Sutherland's (1940) identification of the issue of 'white collar' crime, contains the more telling criticisms of representativeness and official statistics. The suggestion here is that much crime committed by businessmen, government officials and professionals in their occupational roles is unsuspected from records. Nader and Green (1972) suggested that the total time spent in jail by all American businessmen who have ever violated the anti-trust laws was a little under two years (see also Wheeler, 1976). The paucity of prosecution on white collar crime, perhaps more than any other factor, raises questions on the representativeness of official crime statistics, and D. M. Smith (1974) expresses the fear that the judicial system discriminates among acts of criminality in such a way as may serve sectional interests.

Misrepresentation

The concept of misrepresentation, closely related to the work of the sociologists of deviance, is argued on the basis that illegality is defined by a set of societal rules and that the official statistics of crime are primarily a product of the agencies of social control. Hindess (1973) argued that the real value of such statistics lay in their role as indicators of the structure of society and its processes of control. Similarly, I. Taylor, Walton and Young (1973) suggested that criminal statistics reveal the class-organized practice of criminal and legal systems. Kitsuse and Cicourel (1963) were concerned with differences between social conduct which produces a unit of behaviour and the organizational activity which labels this behaviour as deviant, and from a rather different standpoint Carr-Hill and Sterns (1979) argue:

> Certain variables, specifically the detection rate and the intensity of social control (the number of policemen) simultaneously determine, and are determined by, the recorded offence rate . . . we cannot use criminal statistics without asking how events became regarded as offences (p. 311).

On the issue of misrepresentation, therefore, the criticism is focused less on the technical procedures of data collecting than on the initial issue of definition which establishes a criminal class. For many critics, deviance in this context is the normal outcome of individuals seeking to express their diversity and the labelling process which 'produces' criminals is artificial in the sense that it stems from one kind of consensus within a section of society. The extent to which the sociologists of deviance dismiss official statistics on these grounds varies but generally they do not use them. Cicourel (1968), for example, argues that the depiction of offences and offenders is an arbitrary decision of the agents of control, but others recognize the existence of a 'real' crime rate. The issue of misrepresentation is by no means confined to crime data but is a more general facet of the radical critique in the social sciences (Sayer, 1979).

USING CRIME DATA

Whereas there are clearly problems with official criminal statistics, they remain the only relatively comprehensive data source. The caveats are now sufficiently well known for researchers to couch their analyses in limited terms and for those who consider their findings to accept them in qualified ways. Official statistics can be used to portray incidence of known offences and offenders and also to provide a preliminary stage from which more detailed investigation, less dependent on official data can proceed (Herbert and Evans, 1974; Baldwin and Bottoms, 1976). For the remainder of this chapter official statistics will be used to depict broad temporal and regional variations in crime rates.

Temporal trends

Official criminal statistics reveal a long-term consistent trend of increasing crime rates which, despite occasional fluctuations, have tended in the United Kingdom to double over a ten-year period. McClintock and Avison (1968) in an analysis of trends between 1955 and 1965 identified greatest increases among more serious types of crime. The murder rate remained constant but robberies increased by over 300 per cent, and breaking offences by over 200 per cent. Surveys in the United States (Harries, 1974) document similar patterns of sharp increase during the 1960s and 1970s. FBI statistics suggest that between 1966 and 1971, a period in which the overall population increase was 5 per cent, serious crimes increased by around 80 per cent. Crimes of violence showed an increase of 90 per cent over this five-year period, and in England and Wales from 1972 to 1976 increased by 50 per cent from 52 000 to 78 000.

Overall crime figures in the United States tend to dwarf those of other countries even when calculated against population bases. Harries (1980) quotes findings from the National Crime Surveys which estimate 21 million personal victimizations, over 17 million household victimizations, and over 2 million business robberies and burglaries in America in 1975. Some comparison can be made from *Criminal Statistics, 1978* recording 2.5 million indictable offences and 1.5 million motoring or non-indictable offences in England and

Wales. Sharper contrasts can be identified for specific types of offences. In 1976 there were 493 homicides in England and Wales compared with 18 780 in the United States, giving a total thirty-eight times higher for a population only four times larger. New York alone in this year recorded 1622 homicides, Chicago 814 and Detroit 663. The President's Commission in its 1967 report examined crime trends in a number of European countries. Between 1955 and 1965 property crime rates increased by more than 200 per cent in West Germany, the Netherlands, Sweden and Finland, and by over 100 per cent in France and Norway. Rates in Belgium, Denmark and Switzerland remained stable.

Variability in definition and recording practice make comparative studies difficult, but Clinard (1978) has studied Switzerland's low crime rate in an attempt to identify differences with other countries and offers some explanation:

> Several explanations may be advanced for the comparatively lower incidence of ordinary crime in Switzerland. They include the nature of the urbanization process, the citizen's relation to government, the accessibility of firearms, together with the low rate of violent crimes, the criminal justice system, the nature of Swiss youth crime, the more open lines of inter-generational communication, and the low rate of crime among foreign workers (p. 150).

Whether this statement amounts to an explanation is questionable, it clearly intermixes cause and effect but the study does point to some of the sources of crime rates in societal traditions, socio-legal systems and the perceived place of the individual in society.

Table 1.2 contains longer-term trends for England and Wales and shows the accelerating rate of increase. Other temporal trends are related to this pattern. Overall population increases from 1901 to 1978 calculated on a similar basis would yield an index of only 169 by the end year; police strength increased by 29 per cent between 1955 and 1965 (McClintock and Avison, 1968); over a similar period the retail price index moved from 100 to 139, the number of private car licences increased by 172 per cent, and television licences by 158 per cent. Another change in qualitative terms was from a punitive to a reformative penal philosophy. Relationships among these various trends are complex and interrelated and can only be noted here (see, however, Carr-Hill and Sterns, 1979, for a full discussion). McClintock and Avison (1968) attempted to summarize the overall period in five phases:

Phase 1 (1900 to 1914) was the end period of nineteenth-century industrial prosperity and was typified by fairly constant levels of crime with minor fluctuations.

Table 1.2 Crime rates in England and Wales: 1901 to 1978

YEAR	RECORDED INDICTABLE OFFENCES	RATES PER 100 000 POP.	RATE INCREASE 1900 = 100
1901	80 962	249	100
1911	97 171	269	108
1921	103 258	273	110
1931	159 278	399	162
1951	549 741	1 255	504
1961	870 894	1 878	754
1971	1 665 663	3 409	1 369
1978	2 395 757	4 878	1 959

Sources: 1901 to 1921 figures from McClintock and Avison (1968), Table 2.2; 1931 to 1978 figures from *Criminal Statistics 1978*, Table 2.2

Phase 2 (1915 to 1930) witnessed economic upheaval and social unrest and a crime increase of 5 per cent per year.

Phase 3 (1931 to 1948) contained economic crises, political and social upheaval and a crime increase of 7 per cent per year.

Phase 4 (1949 to 1954) was a period of social adjustment and strong fluctuations in crime rate.

Phase 5 (1955 to 1965) was the period of the 'affluent society' and an annual crime increase of 10 per cent.

The somewhat contradictory outcome of this classification is that crime is highest in the most affluent phase of development. Carr-Hill and Sterns (1979) in a critique of this type of analysis conclude that as the key variables of detection rate, offence rate and police strength are all mutually interdependent, no sensible case for 'crime waves' can be made from official statistics. Certainly there are considerable caveats involved. Official statistics are most accurate for more serious offences, which are less likely to escape notice or reporting and allow least discretion. For a range of lesser offences the doubts on reliability of data will remain until more comprehensive reporting of offences by the public and recording by the police lead to a reduction in underrepresentation. Given, however, the semi-autonomous effects of representativeness and misrepresentation, official statistics are unlikely in themselves to be a sufficient basis for the analysis of offences and offenders or indeed of the victims.

Regional patterns in England and Wales

Although there is a considerable amount of information which can be analysed geographically at an aggregate level, the territorial divisions are large and preclude more than a limited amount of interpretation. The patterns which are presented graphically from data in official returns have therefore to be regarded in that context. Figure 1.1 has been compiled from data in the study by McClintock and Avison (1968) in which they classify the 125 contemporary police districts into nine groups based on their ranking by selected indices. Places shown (for 1955 and 1965) have the highest rates of more serious offences. In 1955 most of the larger urban areas, London, Liverpool, Manchester and Newcastle upon Tyne fall within this category along with the smaller cities of Cardiff, Doncaster and Brighton, and the two county forces of Essex and Hertfordshire. By 1965, the emphasis on large city forces is even greater, with all six standard conurbations now included and Cardiff and Doncaster as the only smaller cities.

By the early 1970s, police amalgamation had occurred and only gross inter-regional variations can now be depicted from official returns. Figure 1.2(A) takes the rates for all indictable offences in 1978 and classifies each police district in terms of deviations from the mean offence rate of forty-two police districts (scores for the City and Metropolitan Districts of London are combined). Again, the strongest single indication is of high rates in large urban areas with London and Merseyside in the highest rate category and West Midlands, West Yorkshire and Northumbria in the adjacent class. Lowest scores occur in rural areas, including Dyfed-Powys in Wales, Suffolk in East Anglia and parts of the Midlands. Property offences (Fig. 1.2(B)) show similar patterns except for the fact that rural areas adjacent to large cities no longer show low scores. For both these distributions, crime rates in very large cities, London 7282 and Merseyside 6864, are in fact well above the mean of 4267; these areas also have twice the average burglary rate. Figure 1.3(A) shows burglary patterns in a rather different way, first by using a ranking procedure to classify police districts into sextiles, and secondly by adding a classification based on proportion of total burglaries in England and Wales falling within a particular police district. Highest ranked

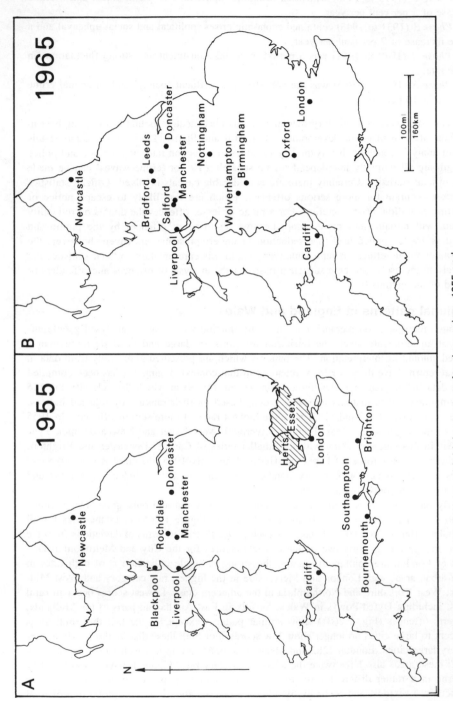

1.1 Police districts in England and Wales with highest rates of serious crime, 1955 and 1965. Source: based on data extracted from McClintock and Avison (1968).

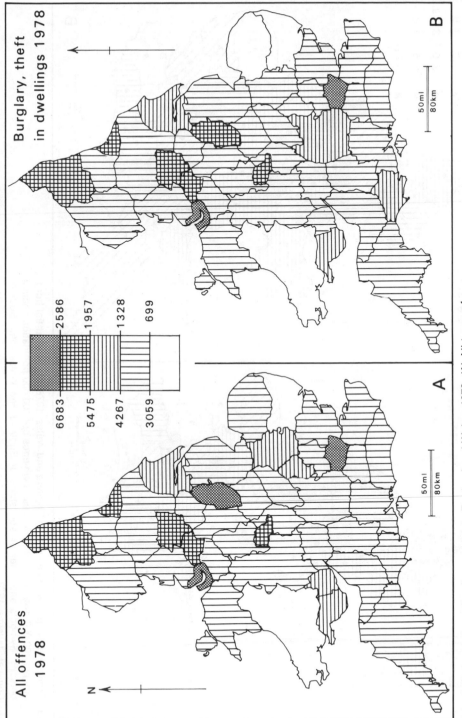

1.2   Crime rates by police force areas in England and Wales, 1978: (A) All types of offences per 100 000 population; (B) Property offences per 100 000 dwellings. Source: *Criminal Statistics*, 1978.

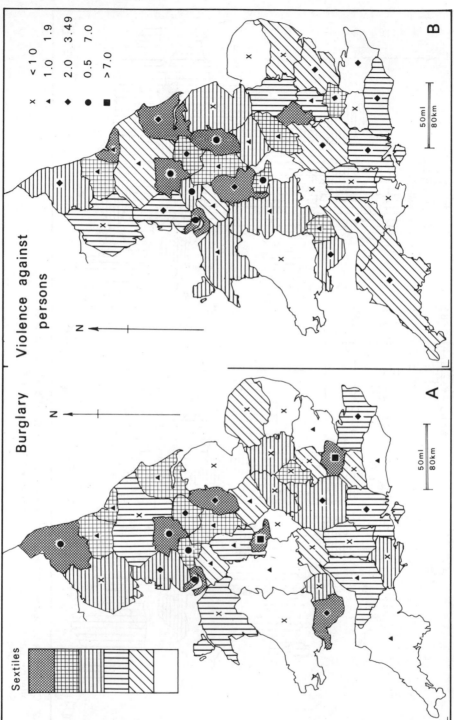

1.3   Crime rates by police force areas in England and Wales, 1978: (A) Residential burglary per 100 000 dwellings; (B) Offences of violence per 100 000 population against
persons. Symbols show percentage share of England and Wales total. Source:
Criminal Statistics, 1978.

areas comprise large cities and urban-industrial regions such as South Wales and Notting-hamshire, districts with a significant rural component fall into the lower rankings. Large cities – especially the six conurbations – absorb high proportions of the total number of burglaries. Figure 1.3(B) adopts the same procedure for offences of violence against persons and here the rankings place less emphasis on the largest cities though in terms of share of total offences they are still dominant. (London contains 16.5 per cent of offences and West Midlands 6.5 per cent).

Criminal Statistics also allow regional variations in the ways that offences are treated in the courts to be depicted. Almost all defendants are initially proceeded against in magis-trates' courts and the period 1954 to 1978 showed a virtually continuous upward trend for both prosecutions and convictions: the 1978 level of proceedings was 2.09 million. About one in six of those found guilty was female and one in five was under seventeen years of age, but account needs to be taken of greater use of police cautioning for juveniles, espe-cially females. Use of formal cautions increased during most of the 1970s though there were large variations among police forces. The range for males aged ten to seventeen years of those cautioned as a proportion of offenders cautioned or otherwise proceeded against in 1978 was from 20 per cent in London, and 28 per cent in South Wales to 67 per cent in Essex; range for violent offenders was from 14 to 50 per cent, and there is *some* consis-tency of police districts by types of offence. A correlation between cautioning rates for all offenders as opposed to violent offenders emerged as +0.48 which was significant at the 1 per cent level; violence and theft, however, yielded an insignificant correlation of +0.28 in terms of rates of caution by police areas. Greater leniency towards females is also reflected in court judgements with 15 per cent of females brought to court receiving a discharge compared to 4 per cent of males.

Sentencing procedures vary with variables such as age group, sex, offence, previous convictions and domestic circumstances. The most common Crown Court sentence for an indictable offence is immediate imprisonment (35 per cent) and for non-indictable offences a fine (36 per cent). Over all types of courts and offences, fines were the most common sanction. Upward trends in sentencing, such as the 50 per cent increase in custodial sen-tences, from 38 000 in 1968 to 57 000 in 1978, must be related to a range of factors, not all of which can be discerned from official statistics. Key considerations which influence sen-tencing cannot be included here but Fig. 1.4 shows variations by police force area in 1978 in the two extreme options: discharges and immediate imprisonment. For males aged ten to seventeen, the average discharge rate is 21 per cent (with a range over districts of 14 to 32 per cent) compared with 5 per cent for males over seventeen years old; the effect of age can therefore be noted together with increased likelihood of previous convictions among older age groups. For the juveniles (Fig. 1.4) there is no clear urban–rural difference in dis-charge rates; London and Merseyside have high rates but not other large cities. Most rural districts, such as Suffolk, Devon, Cumbria and North Yorkshire, have low rates, as do three out of four Welsh forces. The range of imprisonment rates from County Courts by police area is from 30.5 per cent to 53.5 per cent. Regional variations are shown in Fig. 1.4, though both high and low rate areas are diverse in composition.

Data from the ninety-seven Crown Court centres allow a finer-grained analysis and here the indices taken are acquittals and imprisonments. Omitting courts with very few cases, the ranges are from 7.1 to 31.2 per cent for acquittals and 25.5 to 54.5 per cent for immediate imprisonments. Recognizing the existence of many unmeasured intervening var-iables, there is still considerable sentencing variation by Crown Court (see Fig. 1.5). High acquittal rates are found in Liverpool, Birkenhead, Burnley, Swansea and Merthyr, and in several London courts; low rates tend to typify courts in the North-East and much of the Midlands and South-West England. For prison sentences, high-rate courts include Manches-

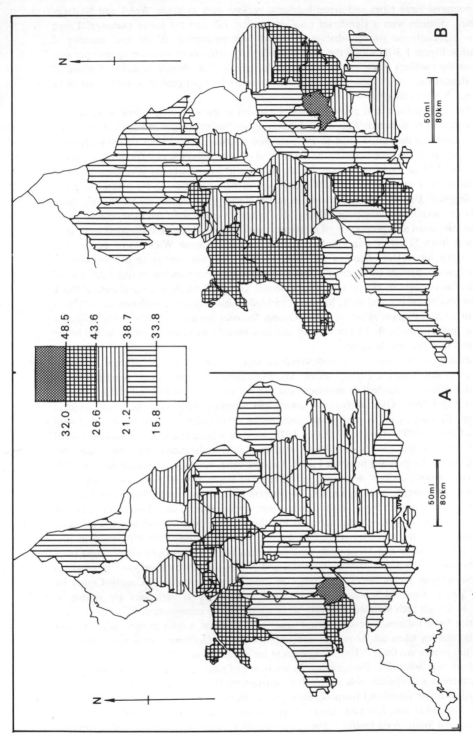

1.4   Sentencing variations by police force areas in England and Wales, 1978: (A) Absolute and conditional discharges in Magistrates' courts; (B) Immediate imprisonments by County Courts. Source: *Criminal Statistics*, 1978.

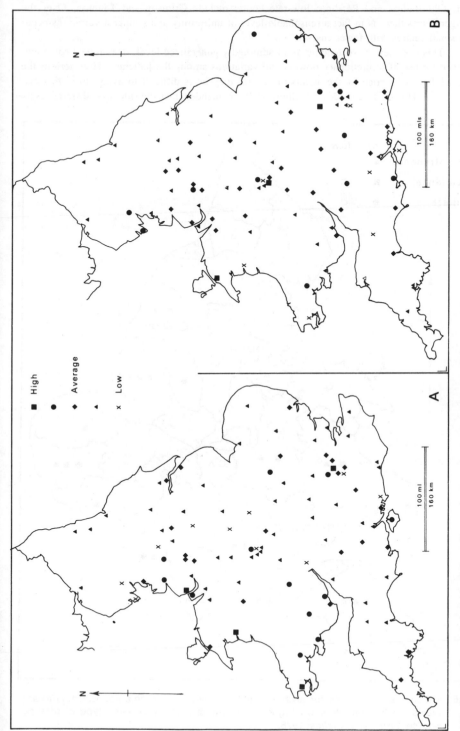

1.5   Sentencing variations by Crown Courts in England and Wales, 1978: (A) Acquittals;
(B) Immediate imprisonment. Symbols show standard deviations above and below
the mean. Source: *Criminal Statistics*, 1978.

ter, Old Bailey, and Reading; low-rate courts include Grimsby and Taunton. Over the larger courts there is in fact a reasonable level of uniformity and strongest variations occur in small centres with fewer cases.

This overview of sentencing at an admittedly generalized level, does reveal some evidence for use of discretionary powers and variations among the judiciary. How serious the variability of practice by the agents of control may be is difficult to assess from this evidence. A Home Office study (Tarling, 1979) concluded that considerable differences in

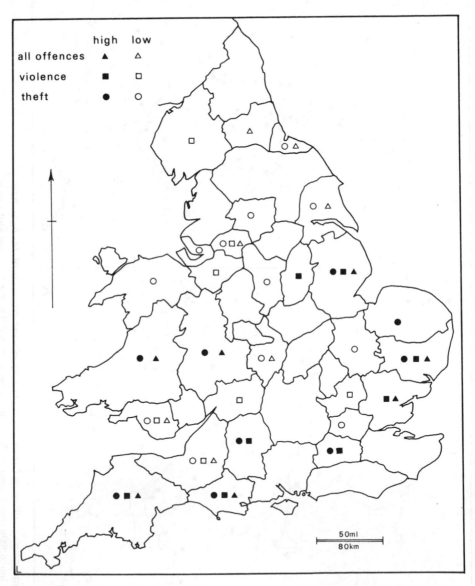

1.6 Police use of cautions for juvenile offenders by police force areas in England and Wales, 1978. Symbols show highest and lowest sextiles for each type of offence. Source: *Criminal Statistics*, 1978.

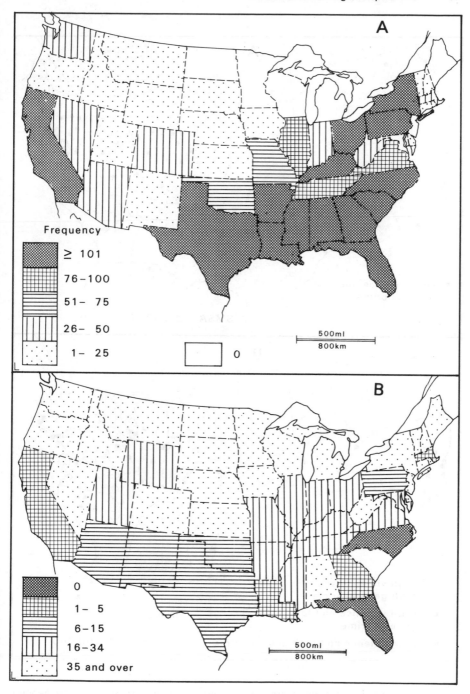

1.7 Homicide in the United States: crime and punishment: (A) Prisoners executed under civil law, 1930 to 1967; (B) Prisoners under sentence of death by jurisdiction, 1974. Source: Harries (1974) p. 104 and Harries and Brunn (1978) p. 29.

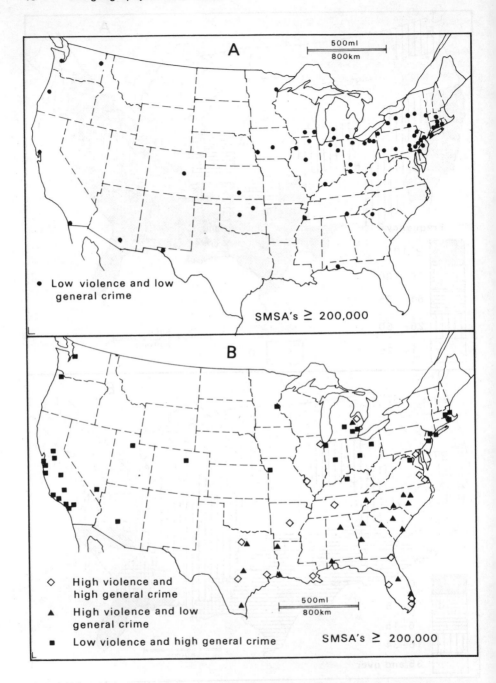

1.8 Crime rates in American metropolitan areas: (A) Low violence and low general crime; (B) High violence and/or high general crime. Categories of S.M.S.A.s are based upon a hierarchical grouping of factor scores. Source: Harries, K.D. (1974), pp. 53–54.

sentencing practice occurred in magistrates' courts and that these differences could not be wholly accounted for in terms of differences in intake and other external factors. Figure 1.6 suggests some link between police use of cautions and magistrates' use of discharge. High caution rates correspond with low discharge rates and a correlation (by police areas) of −0.37, significant at the 5 per cent level, confirms this relationship. The police effectively filter out those with whom the courts are likely to be lenient.

Regional patterns in the United States

In contrast with the very limited amount of attention which has been afforded to regional variations of crime rates in England and Wales, American patterns have now received considerable analysis. Lottier (1938) identified high murder rates in South-eastern states, robbery rates were highest on an axis from Washington to Texas, and larceny rates in the West. Shannon (1954) confirmed the pattern of homicide rates as did Harries (1980) using FBI statistics (see Fig. 1.7). Harries (1974) classified California, New York, Maryland, Nevada and Florida as the most criminogenic states and North Dakota, Mississippi, West Virginia, Vermont and New Hampshire as the least criminogenic. Of attempts to explain regional variations in crime rates, that referring to 'Southern violence' has been most consistent. Harries (1980) reviewed a group of theories all of which revolved around the notion of a 'subculture' based on traditions, cultural development, and contemporary life style. The theory is attractive but very difficult to test empirically.

Most American studies at a below state level tend to identify sharp urban–rural differences and to identify large cities as main problem areas. Haynes (1973) offered the concept of density of opportunity as a key correlate and found some empirical support for this in an analysis of eighty-six American cities. Harries (1980) tested this model and found it useful descriptively but it had little explanatory power. Figure 1.8 classifies American standard metropolitan areas (SMSAs) on the bases of high or low levels of general crime and violent crime. The overrepresentation of violence in southern SMSAs comes out clearly, although there are clusters in California and in older urban-industrial areas of the eastern seaboard and the mid-West. Low rates are most prevalent in the wider North-eastern United States.

Harries and Brunn (1978) have analysed sentencing variations and Fig. 1.9 shows the pattern by judicial districts. These vary from a low sentence weight of 2.6 in Louisiana West to a high of 12.7 in Alabama South. A core area of severe sentences covers central states such as Oklahoma and Kansas, and lenient sentences are most frequent along the Atlantic seaboard. Prisoners under sentence of death in 1974 were most typical of Southern states; in 1976 these states had 42.2 per cent of American homicides and 75.2 per cent of the inmates of death row. Harries and Brunn (1978) identified three broad sets of factors which may influence sentencing disparity – the characteristics of the court, of the defendant, and of the local cultural milieu – which in combination produce 'a sentencing lottery in our nation's courtrooms'.

SUMMARY

This chapter has reviewed some of the main problems associated with official statistics and their use in research; the terms underrepresentation, representativeness, and misrepresentation have been used as headings under which to discuss these issues. These statistics have been used to show regional variations in offences and sentencing but largely in a limited and descriptive way. As bases for explanation, data sources at this aggregate level have little direct value but they can usefully raise questions regarding both the patterns them-

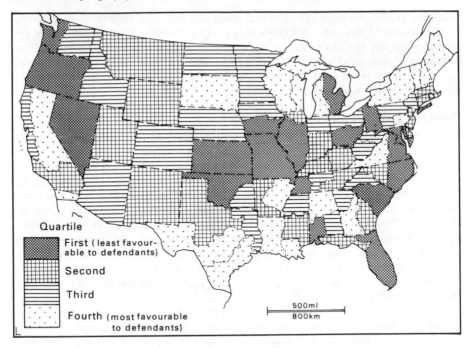

1.9   Mean sentencing weights in American courts, 1970. Source: Harries and Brunn (1978) p. 96.

selves and the ways in which they arise, to which different types of research strategy may be applied. Discussion in this chapter has highlighted those questions – What is a crime? and Who are the criminals? – which have dominated much of the debate in criminology over recent years. Apart from the fact that a crime and a criminal are defined as such by the 'law-makers' at any one point in time, these are questions without resolution. The fact that they are now raised in a persistent manner is important in itself in so far as it ensures that there is a close scrutiny of the ways in which the system works which may be used to monitor its fairness and efficiency.

In this chapter a geography of recorded offences and known offenders, focused on variations among larger cities and police districts, has been drawn from official statistics. This inter-urban and regional scale of analysis has tended to typify many available 'geographies' of crime (Harries, 1974). At this scale some interesting observations on variations over space can be made and broad correlations can be noted, but the aggregate nature of the data are such as to hide detailed variations and differences between sub-areas or small towns within the larger police districts. For the remainder of this book, most reported analyses will be at the intra-urban scale in an attempt to develop more detailed forms of investigation and also to focus more closely on the methodological links between social geography and criminology.

CHAPTER 2
CRIMINOLOGY AND GEOGRAPHY: THEORIES AND CONCEPTS

INTRODUCTION

Any study of crime and delinquency needs to be set in context not only within the methodology of its own discipline but also within the framework of the theoretical development of criminology. There are parallels between the more recent experience of human geography and the methodological changes which have affected criminological research; one effect of the parallelism, almost convergence, is to give more common features than have existed in the past. Criminology has contained alternative perspectives over a long period, and West (1967) is probably correct in suggesting that one weakness of the social theories of delinquency has been the absence of factual evidence in support of one perspective rather than another. Of the two broad divisions in terms of theory-formation, treatment and causation, the former (Klare, 1966) has rather less ambiguity in the sense that alternative approaches can be tested and monitored. Yet little consensus on the issues of the 'treatment debate', such as punitive or reformative deterrents, has emerged and there is considerable variety in actual practice from one society to another. Causation theory – Why does an individual become an offender? – is particularly riven with discords and failure to prove the value of any single-stranded theories led to the so-called multifactor solutions in the 1960s. Most of these causation theories looked for evidence either among groups of known offenders or in local circumstances from which they emerged. The situation was further complicated in the 1970s with the emergence of the school of the sociology of deviance.

This new perspective questioned not simply the details of a particular concept but the whole set of premises upon which 'traditional' criminology was based. Phillipson (1971) argued that from a sociological perspective, the history of criminology had been a history of failure:

> To take crime out of its social context and to try and explain it as the product of a minority of unfortunate individuals apparently *outside* the bounds of conventional society has been a cardinal sin of traditional criminology (p. 24).

The alternative approaches developed in the 1970s offer major new perspectives which are in large part radical and often Marxist, in contradiction to the traditional theories with their positivist and functionalist overtones. A further strand based on symbolic interaction is again in sharp contrast to traditional positions and the emerging sets of theories or 'competing paradigms' (Eisenstad and Curelaru, 1976) contribute to an eclecticism in which coexistence is difficult.

> Intellectual disarray can arise when different styles of logic are exposed to one another in an unregulated fashion. Functionalist criminology does not lend itself to marriage

with Marxism. Structuralism has little in common with symbolic interactionism. Such criminologies cannot easily be matched (Rock, 1979, p. 75)

Rock's plea is for a commonsense perspective on deviance which focuses on the victims and the discomfort they suffer from criminal acts. Here he shares some common ground with Carr-Hill and Sterns (1979) who would also look at the agents of control rather than the 'offenders'. Deviance theories are clearly opposed to traditional theories, but it is important to stress that both are umbrella terms which cover a variety of individual concepts. In reviewing the emergence of traditional theories, some of this variety will become apparent.

THE DEVELOPMENT OF CRIMINOLOGICAL THEORIES

The diversity which exists among traditional criminological theories arises primarily from the long timespan over which concepts have evolved and these tend to reflect broader shifts within the social sciences as a whole. The 'classical' school, most closely associated with Beccaria (1764: 1953 repr.), was founded during the early part of the nineteenth century. Strongly related to the doctrine of free will, it sought to reduce punishment for criminal offences and in this sense predated modern reformative attitudes. This perspective was replaced by essentially positivist approaches which established a framework for later theories. The common features of these theories included assumptions of consensus as a fact of society, the determination of personal and environmental forces, and the adaptation of more scientific and often quantitative methods. Early branches had an overtly crude determinism. Lombroso (1875: 1968 repr.) was a founding father of biological determinism in the latter part of the nineteenth century in a criminology now closely concerned with the causation of crime. He argued that criminal tendencies were hereditary and that 'born criminals' could be identified by their distinctive physical characteristics. In their simplest mechanistic form, these theories were discounted at an early period, but versions of biological determinism have persisted. Sheldon (1949) reported that two-thirds of a group of Boston delinquents had a high level of muscular and body tissue; the Gluecks (1950; 1952) continued to measure individual physiological traits with their somato-typing procedures. Other psychological positivists (Trasler, 1963) have similarly extended this technique to measure the mental features of known offenders.

Some early work on the influences of physical environment on criminal behaviour can be noted. There were studies relating climatic variations and seasonality to crime (Harries, 1980) with a frequent assertion that an increase in violent crimes took place during the summer and in property offences during the winter. Whereas statistical associations of this kind exist, they rarely stand up to close examination and at best reflect variations in opportunities. An independent effect from a natural environmental phenomenon has yet to be demonstrated.

As environmental factors entered the criminological literature the measures adopted were social, economic and man-made rather than natural or physical. The ecology of the Chicago school (Shaw and McKay, 1942) stimulated many of these approaches. Shaw and McKay were influenced by the broader ecological theories but their own work was concerned with juvenile delinquency in particular and had strong social work connotations. Using delinquency rates calculated for community areas in Chicago and other American cities, they found consistent correlations with indices of mobility, housing quality, poverty, unemployment and ethnic minority groups. They argued that these correlates had no special causal implications but were themselves, along with high delinquency rates, symptoms of some underlying condition from which deviant behaviour might emerge. The theory of social disorganization was developed from this basis and suggested that in the absence of a stable form of society with legalistically based codes of behaviour and established norms and values, precipitating conditions for criminality would exist. The theory predicts, therefore, large numbers of offenders in areas and among groups which are typified by social disorganization. Critics of the theory (Mays, 1963) argue that it fails to account for high delinquency rates in stable, 'organized', inner-city districts but the concept continues to receive attention (Baldwin and Bottoms, 1976).

The influential concept of anomie, originally associated with Durkheim and the notion of normlessness, has also been used in attempts to explain criminal behaviour. Durkheim (1: 1966) showed how rapid economic and social change would lead to a certain level of deviance and suggested that those groups who were subject to most violent change, either in terms of their economic situation or in terms of their value patterns, were the most likely to deviate. Merton (1938) took a static situation rather than one of change and examined the efforts of individuals to attain socially prescribed goals. Whereas it could be argued that both anomie and social disorganization could be linked to territories within large cities, neither was developed primarily in relation to local environmental circumstances. Both sought to relate an individual's disposition towards criminality to underlying *structural* conditions; it was the nature of the encompassing societal system and the individual's place within it which formed the main point of reference.

Shaw and McKay were also associated with the theory of cultural transmission in which the delinquent tradition, 'nurtured' among some sections of society, could again be viewed in a territorial context. H. Mayhew's (1862) description of rookeries in London, where children were born and bred to the business of crime, is closely related to this notion of delinquent behaviour being transmitted over time and space. Sutherland's (1940) theory of differential association, which suggests that a person becomes delinquent because of an excess of definitions favourable to violations of law over definitions favourable to law, also has common features. 'Definitions' include attitudes and techniques; frequency and nature of contacts are also clearly of central importance. The steps from theories of this kind, which tend to view the offender in local circumstances, to the subcultural theories which dominated a couple of decades from the later 1950s, were short. L. Taylor (1973) regarded the subculturalists as inheritors of the Chicago tradition and Phillipson (1971) suggested that theories such as anomie, social disorganization and cultural transmission, all provided the basis for a subcultural approach.

A subculture suggests the existence of identifiable groups within which particular sets of knowledge, beliefs, values and normative codes of behaviour are typical. The concept of a delinquent subculture arises from the fact that some of the elements associated with such a group may be illegal and at odds with those adopted by the wider society. Matza (1964) described subcultural theory as a 'modern rendition of positivism' in which peer groups form reference groups establishing behavioural norms. There are, as Hood and Sparks (1970) suggest, variants on the theory of subculture. Miller (1958) generalized from his analyses of lower-class youths and saw delinquency as part of their traditional behaviour or one of their 'focal concerns'. Downes (1966) appears to find some support for this interpretation from his studies of British youths. Cohen (1955) and Cloward and Ohlin (1960) saw subcultural delinquency as a reaction by working-class youths to their failure to achieve in middle-class terms. Broadly, their contention is that delinquency is the collective solution of young, lower-class males placed in a situation of stress; a situation in which opportunities for advancement through legitimate channels are blocked. Whereas Cohen envisaged an oppositional attitude to middle-class values, Cloward and Ohlin emphasized the availability to the adolescent of both illegitimate and legitimate opportunities; delinquency was not a reaction to middle-class standards but a refusal to legitimize them. For Cloward and Ohlin, the content of a delinquent subculture was significantly shaped by its local milieu, and they classified the various responses in that milieu as criminal, conflict and retreatist.

Matza (1964) emphasized the extent to which subcultures could be integrated with the surrounding social world; delinquents are not isolated but are encircled by institutions which uphold conventional values. For Matza most young offenders retain choice, and 'drift' between conventional and delinquent behaviour; they rationalize deviance in terms unacceptable to society but are capable of reform.

Subcultural theory again has some particular interest for social geographers, as local environment can be abstracted as one framework for behaviour. The extent to which groups have been linked with territories within the city is variable, but for most theorists these were not central features. Cohen (1955) and Cloward and Ohlin (1960) focused on lower-class youth in a gang context and showed very limited awareness of spatial connotations, although the association of such groups with 'turfs' or territories is well-established. Links with more closely researched themes by geographers occur with concepts such as neigh-bourhood and 'community' within which localized sets of values and norms can be hypothesized. Subcultural theory has some attractions, therefore, in that it can be theorized in spatial terms, groups can be identified with places. Subculture as a concept also has more flexibility than many other positivist stances. It can accommodate the fact that many 'non-delinquents' are found in delinquency areas (Cloward and Ohlin, 1960), it includes the function of free will, drift and choice (Matza, 1964) and it provides many attractions as a working hypothesis for geographers focusing upon the intervening effects of local environ-ments.

The sociology of deviance

The sociological theories of deviance have provided emphatic moves away from the positiv-ist and correctional stances of many traditional perspectives. These theories focus on social controls and definitions, and on criminal law and the judicial system, rather than on offen-ders. The development of this radical critique led to the 'new' criminology of the 1970s and the institutional rifts (Wiles, 1976) following the establishment of the National Deviancy Conference in 1968. Between the traditional theories and the new radical perspectives, labelling theory and symbolic interactionism were interposed and these assumed special roles.

> Labelling theory is perhaps best seen as a transitional stage in the move from tradi-tional criminology to the new criminologies, but this status is frequently obscured by the fact that the institutional rift between old and new criminologies centred on issues raised by labelling theory (Wiles, 1976, p. 14).

Wiles is critical of the way in which labelling theory has been developed in British deviance studies, describing it as crude and simplistic. A key notion of labelling theory is that social groups 'create' deviance by making rules and labelling violators of these rules as deviant. Whereas this approach posed new questions (which ironically it could not answer) it was not radical in itself but it did (Wiles, 1976) have two concerns which seeded the new, radical criminologies. Firstly, the deviant became viewed as an actor whose actions were a consequence of an interpretation of the world and, secondly, criminology had to acknowledge the explanatory roles of laws and rules and their political nature. Positivist criminology took law, the legislators and the enforcers as given, and effectively adopted a conservative political stance which preserves the *status quo*. The new criminology sees the determinants of criminal law and behaviour as political power relationships which emanate from the process of production. Whereas functional theorists see the law as an outcome of consensus in a value-neutral state, concerned with 'criminals', rehabilitation and the crime problem, conflict theorists see social control as an outcome of unequal distributions of economic and political power in which laws serve the dominant classes.

One outcome of this critique has been a new criminology which has a variety of strands but is nevertheless in total opposition to both traditional positivism and social reaction: For us, as for Marx . . . deviance is normal in the sense that men are consciously involved in asserting their human diversity . . . the task is to create a society in which the facts of human diversity whether personal, organic or social, are not subject to the power to criminalize (I. Taylor *et al.*, 1973, p. 282).

This argument suggests that capitalist society views criminal behaviour as essentially 'street crime', committed by people of low socio-economic status and the law has been developed with excessive attention paid to the need to protect property. For Marxists the roots of problems lie in the private ownership of the means of production and the inequalities which this situation produces. Critics of Marxism in this context point to a weak record of empirical research and idealistic stances; Wiles (1976), however, argues that this is an inevitable stage following the rejection of an established and monolithic paradigm.

METHODOLOGICAL DEVELOPMENTS IN HUMAN GEOGRAPHY

This review of the theories of criminology and deviance has necessarily been brief and fuller discussions are available elsewhere (Mannheim, 1965; I. Taylor *et al.*, 1973; Nettler, 1974). In relating these theories to human geography, a first observation must be that a strong parallelism exists in terms of contemporary trends (Herbert and Johnston, 1978). As a series of paradigmatic shifts have located criminology more firmly within the focal concerns of the social sciences, similar developments have affected human geography. During the 1950s and 1960s, human geography became centrally concerned with explicitly positivist modes of analysis often linked with model-building and quantitative methods. The spatial analysis phase provided important methodologies and techniques, at least for geographers *per se* who were concerned with identifying patterns at regional and intra-urban scales. As the emphasis in terms of analysis shifted from pattern to process and 'response' (Herbert, 1980b), much of this methodology retained its usefulness. Reactions to spatial analysis with its positivistic qualities began to appear at the end of the 1960s and bore strong similarities to those experienced in criminology. There was an intermediary phase between positivist and 'radical' perspectives but if anything this was less adequately theorized than in criminology.

Initial interest in behavioural processes were couched in positivist terms and the much later shift to 'humanistic' geography focused on qualitative and subjective facets of human behaviour. Interests in cognitive mapping, environmental perception and the values and meanings attached to place introduced facets of symbolic interactionism, but in a weakly developed conceptual framework. Radical geography (Peet, 1977) initiated a strong attack on functionalism and the conservative bases of positive science but had similar disregard for what it termed the reductionist tendencies of humanistic geography. Radical geography, with its strong Marxist connotations provides a critique but not as yet a convincing record of empirical research. As humanistic geography seeks to establish its theoretical bases (Ley, 1977) and spatial analysis to reassert its value (Hay, 1979), an eclecticism which shows few trends towards integration begins to typify human geography.

Radical geography has brought a clear awareness of the need to acknowledge and investigate levels of analysis other than the local environment which has been the geographer's conventional concern. Despite this awareness most empirical work in human geography continues to focus upon pattern, process and response in local environment as the spatial outcomes of a societal system. Most available 'geographies' of crime discussed in this book are firmly cast in this mould. Even at this stage, however, a research strategy can be outlined for the 'geography' of crime which both sets different approaches in their relative position within the overall framework and sets some context for the crucial task of integrating various 'scales' of analysis.

A FRAMEWORK FOR A GEOGRAPHY OF CRIME

This framework affords space a central position and recognizes the roles of more conventional analysis shown in Fig. 2.1 level 3 (Consumption). It also relates space to what are essentially production and distribution functions in levels 1 (Production) and 2 (Distribution), and suggests that it is from these 'roots' of the system, its ideologies and allocative systems, that any manifestations in space originate. As the geography of crime has developed (Harries, 1974; 1980; Pyle *et al.*, 1974) it has been contexted almost exclusively in the third level of analysis. Regional patterns have been identified, the broad spatial ecology of offences and offenders has been displayed through detailed correlative exercises, and some of the humanistic qualities of local places have been studied. This research record will be examined in chapters which follow. Levels 1 and 2 possess no empirical research record of note but it is essential at this stage to assess their place in a research strategy for crime and to relate this to changing perspectives in human geography as a whole.

As radical geography emerged in the 1970s it had strong links with Marxism. As Marxism itself has many interpretations, often competing, and as some radical geographers used other theoretical bases, 'critique' is rather more diffuse and variegated than a label

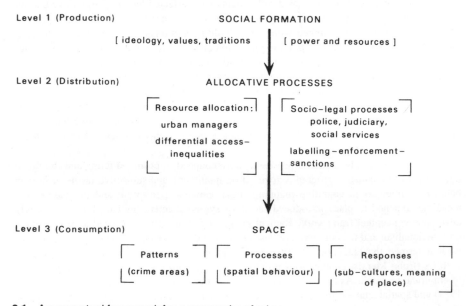

2.1   A conceptual framework for a geography of crime.

such as radical geography might suggest. Perhaps the most impressive role of this critique to date has been that of a catalyst for the development of alternative viewpoints and as a thrust towards greater involvement with the philosophies of the social sciences. As the Marxist perspective develops it is less an explicit call for the acceptance of ideological stances of a specific kind than an argument for a partiuclar type of methodology capable of analysing society. The intellectual appeal of Marxism rests on its theoretical bases and the conceptual framework which it provides for the analysis of social phenomena. In his commentary on available geographies of crime Peet (1975; 1976) offered first a critique and second an alternative research strategy. The critique, which though directed at analysis of crime was equally applicable to any other social problem, did raise similar key questions to those identified by the sociologists of deviance in their attack upon traditional criminology. These included the superficiality of some spatial research, the need to research the origins of inequalities in the class structure of society, and the role of present studies in maintaining the *status quo*. These are some of the central issues for the first level of analysis in what remains a critique rather than a 'constructive' research perspective. Peet's statement to the effect that the geography of crime is the predictable spatial manifestation of contradictions inherent in the capitalist mode of production deserves close and serious attention.

Peet's own proposal for a radical theory of lower-class crime, though explicitly preliminary, does not take us very far in either theoretical or pragmatic terms. It tends in itself to be a somewhat superficial and mechanistic account of the conditions which produce criminality. These are general precipitating circumstances of the type which have been rejected many times, largely because they fail to explain the differential responses to these circumstances. Poverty, disadvantage and even social disorganization have been recognized as 'conditions' out of which delinquency emerges; a radical theory takes us one step back and sees the origins of poverty and disadvantage in the class-based mode of production, but it still takes us no further towards understanding why from 'shared' circumstances some individuals will become delinquent and others will not. The dimension concerned with agencies of control who make the rules and define the offenders needs to be added, but this basic fact of differential response at an individual level remains and still needs research at a local level where cultural differences and a host of intervening variables are involved.

For the moment, therefore, Peet's (1976) prescriptions for a new geography of crime have little attraction; more generally, radical geography has focused attention on the first level of analysis and the case to context analyses of social problems in these broader terms is proven. A number of other elements of the critique can also be accepted with some qualifications. First of these is the contention that crime is a surface manifestation of discontents which lie deeply embedded in the social system, and that any study which starts, continues and ends at the surface cannot possibly deal with cause. Second is the contention that the geography of crime is actually the geography of lower-class crime; those in power may collect statistics in their own interest. This criticism is the general point on official statistics which has been fully discussed in Chapter 1 and needs some qualification. Third is the accusation levelled at a liberal geography of crime, suggesting that by its focus on management and control it acts as a think-tank for a protective bureaucracy. In general terms this is now a well-rehearsed argument. Liberal geographers argue that much can be accomplished by working with and within the system, radical geographers that the system generates more problems than can be cured without a commitment to fundamental change. These differences must revolve around a value judgement on the quality of the 'system' *per se*. Similarly, a fourth contention that crime is a predictable outcome of modern capitalism must ultimately be resolved by value judgements and ideological interpretations.

At this first level of analysis, therefore, conventional geographies of crime, typically weak in terms of theoretical bases and with no worthwhile empirical research record, need to accommodate and respond to a critique which has many telling qualities. Virtually identical experience in criminology has led to institutional rifts and an eclecticism in which alternative perspectives coexist but do not interact. To the extent that the positions are developed in human geography the eclecticism and apparent incompatibility can be discerned. What Fig. 2.1 offers is a framework within which the relationships among different scales or levels of analysis can be recognized. What no diagram can do is to show ways in which different theoretical positions can be reconciled and integrated. This issue is especially relevant at the first level of analysis, though it does apply elsewhere, and some comments are pertinent. Firstly, in a situation recognized by Eisenstad and Curelaru (1976) of 'competing paradigms', there is some general need for 'openings' and rather more flexible positions from which a meaningful dialogue can develop. Secondly, there are core positions which are not reconcilable and difference as such should be recognized. A great deal is to be said for applying different perspectives to the same empirical problem and examining results in a comparative framework. The least acceptable solution would be to select concepts from different frameworks in an *ad hoc* and atheoretical way. A related approach would be that of more systematic comparative analysis of societies with different political economies, such as capitalist and socialist states.

Allocative systems, designated as the second level of analysis in Fig. 2.1, again offer a theme with a very limited research tradition in human geography. Although geographers became interested in managerialism, particularly in the context of the housing market, during the 1970s, much of this work could be labelled as empiricist and adequate theories did not emerge. Pahl (1979) and Saunders (1980) have now offered useful conceptual guidelines and the roles of urban managers or 'gatekeepers' and their place in the system are clearly worthy of close attention. Most theories, including Marxism, recognize the existence of managers as decision-makers, the issue concerns the relative autonomy of their roles, their discretionary powers and the rationality upon which their decisions are based. As Fig. 2.1 suggests, general features of distribution involving the unequal allocation of resources and thus of disadvantage are relevant but it is the parallel set of managers concerned with the socio-legal system which is of direct interest to the study of crime. Interposed between the social formation and the offender is a large number of individuals including the judicial hierarchy from Law Lords to local magistrates, the legal profession in its prosecution and defence roles, and the enforcing and reformative agencies of police, welfare services and penal institutions.

There is a substantial criminological literature on the socio-legal system and the ways in which it works. Sentencing disparity, for example, has received close attention (Lemon, 1974; Tarling, 1979) and the effects of various forms of sanctions and deterrents have been closely monitored and debated (Carr-Hill and Sterns, 1979). These studies, including some work by geographers (Harries and Brunn, 1978), provide clear examples of variations within the socio-legal system and differential uses of discretionary powers. Research of this kind provides some insight into the managerial framework and its outcomes, but considerable scope exists for further study at this second level of analysis. There are numerous key issues to be identified. Social definition of the rules and laws which identify offenders have been insufficiently scrutinized; whose interests do they serve? what sections of society are they directed against? Discretion is considerable and increases the further down the hierarchy one descends to the officer 'on the beat'; How is such discretion exercised? Upon what premises is it based? Spatial outcomes of discretion may be identified but the ways in which the courts operate in regional contexts and the manner in which police allocate their resources over space remain largely unresearched. Is there a theory of managerialism within which the decision-making procedures which occur within the socio-legal system can be set?

SUMMARY

As a geography of crime develops, it can have no separate existence either from criminology or from human geography. It looks to the former for evolving theoretical bases and conceptual positions and for much of its crime-specific research literature, it looks to the latter for basic methodologies to which it can relate. A geography of crime will retain a strong descriptive role which depicts patterns in space, and here there is room to revise and improve ways in which the roles of space and place have been incorporated into criminological research. There are deeper analytical roles which can be developed, though most geographers would admit that spatial processes in themselves are rarely explanatory processes and it is always necessary to probe deeply into social, political and economic forces at various levels of analysis. This may take us some way towards a unified social science perspective on criminological issues, but it is more likely that geographers will retain their disciplinary label and identity while working in increasingly overlapping orbits with others to their mutual benefit and hopefully those of the phenomena – offenders, victims, and agents of control – they seek to analyse.

CHAPTER 3
AREAL AND ECOLOGICAL APPROACHES TO THE STUDY OF CRIME

INTRODUCTION

Although criminological research reaches back over some two centuries, professional geographers have not been directly involved until the very recent past. In the 1970s Scott (1972) could describe his own interest in crime and delinquency as evidence of 'geographical deviance'. This non-involvement reflects prevailing paradigms and research priorities within geography rather than any intrinsic lack of interest or applicability, as criminologists consistently recognized some of the spatial qualities of the phenomena which they studied. The environmentalist paradigm of the late nineteenth and early twentieth centuries might have provided a link with the geography of crime, but its scale was inappropriate and its foundations lay solidly in the natural sciences. Again, despite early depiction of crime areas in cities and the general association of crime rates with level of urbanization, urban geography made no early moves to accommodate this kind of study. Historical growth, morphology and economic functions were foci of attention and even as the interest in social geography of cities gathered momentum in the 1960s, its initial emphases were on macro-patterns and processes and residential differentiation. It was not really until the behavioural dimension had been added and questions of relevance had been raised in their modern forms that the terms of reference of urban geography were such that topics such as crime and delinquency could be counted as legitimate research themes. Along with topics such as education, mental illness and deprivation, crime could be researched in a social geography of widening intellectual horizons and, in common with these topics, it represented a real and relevant societal problem.

Despite this neglect by geographers *per se*, criminology contains ample awareness of the significance of spatial factors and even before the spatial ecology of the 1920s there were consistent attempts to relate crime rates to areas and specific forms of urban environment and to examine their distributional qualities.

NINETEENTH-CENTURY VIEWS: REGIONAL DIFFERENCES AND CRIMINAL AREAS

Both Phillips (1972) and Sutherland and Cressey (1970) have referred to a 'cartographic' school of criminology which existed from 1830 to 1880, being initiated in France and spreading to England and other European countries. New sources of official data on crime rates and their variation over time and by regions provided a powerful stimulus to research of this kind. The adjective 'cartographic' arises from the frequent use of maps to show regional variations in crime rates and particularly urban-rural differences. Ecological association formed part of the analysis in the sense that the relationships of crime rates with other indicators of social condition were measured and discussed. Guerry (1833) used a series of annual reports to analyse French crime patterns and found consistent regional differences modified by factors such as seasonality. For example, crimes against property had a higher incidence in the north during winter, whereas crimes against persons reached highest levels in the south during the summer. This particular finding pointed towards some climatic factor of relevance but Guerry also examined the effects of population

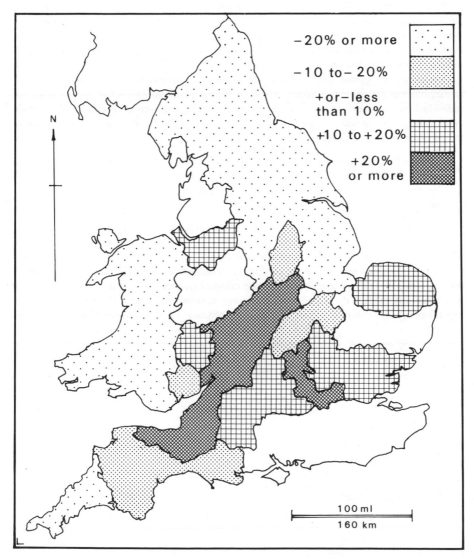

3.1 Patterns of crime in England and Wales at mid-nineteenth century: an example of the cartographic school. Based upon commitments of males to Assize and Quarter Sessions 1842–47; shows proportions above and below the mean with weighting by age of population. Source: Fletcher (1849).

density and education. Here the incidence of property crimes seemed related to urban areas, to wealth and to highest levels of literacy. Such findings commit most of the sins of ecological fallacy but had some descriptive value.

Fletcher (1849) provided a similar analysis of English crime statistics (Fig. 3.1). He again found high crime rates in generally wealthier counties but recognized these as 'collecting' rather than 'breeding' areas for criminals, showing some awareness of the factor of opportunities. Fletcher's finding that high crime rates typified agricultural rather than manufacturing counties has proved eccentric in the context of this type of literature. H. Mayhew (1862), for example, showed variations by population density and fourteen measures of deviant behaviour over the counties of England and Wales, and concluded that crime was most frequent in areas of industrial and urban character. Scott (1972) summarizes findings from several parts of the world which show a link between urbanization and crime and this remains a persistent feature at this scale of analysis.

Whereas the cartographic school was mainly concerned with regional patterns of crime, other contemporary accounts focus on the crime areas which had emerged within individual cities. The so-called 'rookeries' were found, for example, in most large British cities during the first half of the nineteenth century (Fig. 3.2). Descriptions such as those of the St Giles district in London were commonplace:

> The nucleus of crime in St Giles consists of about six streets, riddled with courts, alleys, passages and dark entries, all leading to rooms and smaller tenements . . . the lowest grade of thieves and dissolute people live in the immediate neighbourhood of the station house (Tobias, 1967, p. 131).

Elsewhere, Tobias identified particular streets, such as the appropriately named Twisters Lane, in which nine-tenths of the population was estimated to be illegally employed. Strange (1980) has reconstructed a detailed portrait of the district of Merthyr known in this period as 'China' in which thieves, prostitutes, vagrants and the dissolute lived in conditions of squalor. Districts such as these were criminal quarters in a total sense; the law had little authority within them and strangers were reluctant to enter. Their context was a rapidly emerging industrial society in which the physical form of urbanization was running

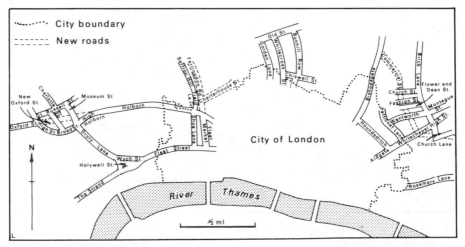

3.2 The 'rookeries' of London in the mid-nineteenth century. Source: Tobias (1967) p. 132.

ahead of an adequate system for the distribution of resources (Stedman-Jones, 1971). The worst areas disappeared during the latter part of the nineteenth century as the reform movement, aimed at improving the living conditions, gathered force, with its assault on overcrowding and public health. Changes in the size and efficiency of the police force were also relevant though for Strange (1980) the main cause for the disappearance of Merthyr's 'China' was economic. As industrial fortunes declined, the police force expanded and 'respectability' became more entrenched, the criminals deserted Merthyr and their crime area gradually dissolved. Clearly the timing and extent of the disappearance of the rookeries varied considerably from one city to another; in some cities vestiges of the old order persisted into the twentieth century.

Mayhew (1862) provided more systematic studies of intra-urban variations in crime rates. Using statistics for each of the seven police districts in London in the mid-nineteenth century, he showed that two of these districts contained two-thirds of known criminals. Other information on average income, tax and poor law assessments allowed him to classify the districts and he was also able to disaggregate the offenders and show clusters of particular types of crime. Throughout the nineteenth century, therefore, a general geography of crime in European countries was known. Regional variations had been identified and measured, crime areas within cities were part of the common knowledge of magistracy and police, and indeed most of the general public.

SPATIAL ECOLOGY FROM THE CHICAGO SCHOOL

The spatial ecology of crime was developed most fully in the 1920s and 1930s with the work in America of Clifford Shaw and Henry McKay. Their best known study (Shaw and McKay, 1942) contained delinquency data on Chicago, collected as part of the Illinois crime survey, and demonstrated a set of techniques which they subsequently extended to other American cities. For the Chicago area they mapped the homes of juvenile offenders brought before the Cook County court at various periods during the first half of the twentieth century. Analysis of these was set in a spatial framework of square-mile grids, concentric zones, and seventy-five designated community areas. Area rates were based on appropriate populations-at-risk and a number of spatial generalizations were identified. A range of cartographic procedures was used, including dot maps to show actual distributions and rate maps to show areal variations, and the generalizations focused on the observation of regular change from centre to periphery. The four main forms of deviance recorded – juvenile delinquency, adult crime, recidivism and truancy – were closely interrelated. Truancy, regarded as a good indicator of potential delinquency, was most typically found in areas adjacent to Chicago's central business district and inner city industrial areas, as was delinquency itself. Adult offenders were more likely to come from rooming house districts of the zone in transition. Overall rates depicted by gradients and zones (Fig. 3.3A) reveal the regular progression from centre to periphery. Replication of the procedure for nineteen other American cities confirmed the spatial model, though two (apparently explicable) deviant sets of results were found in Baltimore and Omaha. A revised version of the original study (Shaw and McKay, 1969) added data sets from the 1960s which showed a persistence of the general pattern, though there was an outward migration of crime rates in one sector, paralleling movements in the black district (Fig. 3.3B).

The areal generalizations were complemented by ecological analyses which correlated variables such as substandard housing, poverty, foreign-born population, and mobility, with high delinquency rates. The broad contrast observed was between central districts of poverty and physical deterioration, whose inhabitants were transient and possessed confused

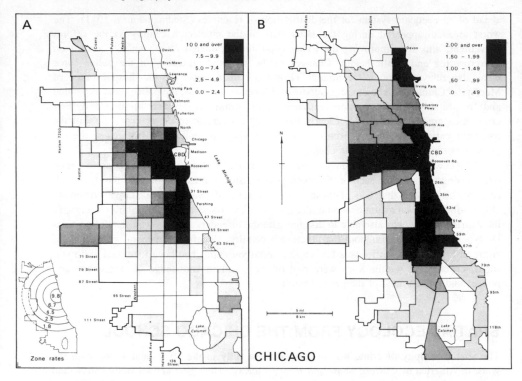

3.3 Juvenile delinquency in Chicago: (A) 1927/33 showing generalized zones and gradients; (B) 1963/66. For 1927–33 rates per 100 males aged 10–16; for 1963–66 rates expressed in terms of a grand mean of 1.00. Source: Shaw and McKay (1969) pp. 54, 69 and 355.

cultural standards, and the more stable family suburbs in which delinquency was invariably low. As Shaw and McKay conceived a delinquency area it emerged from the transmission of delinquent behaviour to a point at which it dominated the attitudes and behaviour of the majority resident in a particular district. In addition to neighbourhood, other social group influences, such as those of family, school and play-group, were recognized and detailed individual case histories of known offenders (Shaw, 1930) were used to supplement more aggregate analyses. The work in Chicago in the interwar period established an ecological tradition in criminology and also provided a significant perspective to which geographies of crime could be related.

Subsequent American studies, including additional work on Chicago, have tended to confirm the persistence of generalized areal patterns as identified by Shaw and McKay. Variations which appear can be related to adjustments in the underlying social geography of the American city, such as the appearance of peripheral industrial areas, though the main feature remains the central city/suburban dichotomy (Cox, 1973). Major technical developments have involved procedures used to measure ecological association, though again results have not been markedly different from those recorded in earlier studies. Lander (1954) used a number of multivariate techniques in his analysis of 8464 cases of juvenile delinquency in Baltimore during the period 1939 to 1942, an analysis which also included a set of census variables composed of measures such as socio-economic status, demographic structure, overcrowding and quality of housing. A factor analysis produced two dimensions. One, which linked crime rates with proportions of non-whites and renters, was labelled as a dimension of anomie; the other, associated with high rents and educational attainment but low delinquency rates, was a social status dimension. Chilton (1964) and Gordon (1967) in different ways queried Lander's findings and produced alternative interpretations, but the step from a small number of correlations to a concept such as anomie is anyway questionable.

Schmid's (1960) study of Seattle provided one of the most comprehensive spatial ecologies of an American city since the pioneering efforts of Shaw and McKay. Data input for this study comprised 35 000 offences known to the police and 30 000 arrests over the time periods 1949 and 1950/51. This data set was reduced to twenty crime variables to which was added a set of eighteen census variables calculated for each of ninety-three census tracts. Both offence and offender data were used in the analysis, with the justification that to define crime or delinquency areas it is important to know not only where offenders live but also where crime is committed. Schmid's summary statement on the geography of crime in Seattle was that the central segment of the city contained 15.5 per cent of the total population, 47 per cent of offences known to police and 63 per cent of the arrests. Areal generalizations by zones and gradients replicated the earlier model. From a factor analysis the three leading dimensions were successively described as low social cohesion and low family status, low social cohesion and low occupational status, and low family and economic status. Of these, the third dimension, with especially high loadings on unmarried and unemployed males and with the range of crime variables was described as the crime dimension *par excellence*. Scores from this factor located crime areas in Seattle:

> Urban crime areas, including areas where criminals reside and areas where crimes are committed, are generally characterized by all or most of the following factors: low social cohesion, weak family life, low socio-economic status, physical deterioration, high rates of population mobility and personal disorganization (Schmid, 1960, p. 678).

This type of areal and ecological generalization has been replicated in studies of other parts of the world. Burt (1925) mapped juvenile offender rates in London in the early 1920s and showed that highest rates occurred adjacent to central commercial districts, with low rates in the suburbs; the delinquency areas coincided with Mayhew's (1862) 'low neighbourhoods' and Booth's (1891) poverty areas. A succession of studies of Liverpool (Jones, 1934; Castle and Gittus, 1957) revealed clusters of social defects, including crime in the inner areas of the city which contained high levels of immigrant population and overcrowding (Fig. 3.4). Wallis and Maliphant (1967) found broadly similar results in a London study which, however, used a very limited sample base. Studies in Third World countries are rare and somewhat inconsistent. Caplow (1949) found crime gradients to be reversed in Guatemala City with highest rates on the urban periphery; Hayner (1946) found a closer resemblance to the American model in Mexico City though some peripheral clusters existed which corresponded with shanty towns. Mangin (1962) did not find high concentrations of offenders in Lima's shanties, but de Fleur (1967) found these to be major source areas in Cordoba. Clinard (1962) simply related high crime rates to neighbourhoods lacking social cohesion and stability. Any attempt to draw generalizations from studies of Third World cities is fraught with difficulty. The few available studies are based on small sample sizes and large observational units: the adequacy of their data bases is extremely doubtful. Differences in areal patterns from Western countries reflect broader contrasts in the social geography of the city whereas general ecological correspondence with poverty and disadvantage is more consistent, though at different scales.

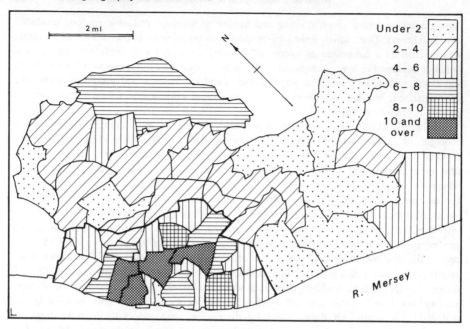

3.4 Patterns of juvenile delinquency in Liverpool, 1936. Rates per 1000 population aged under 21 years. Source: Bagot (1940) p. 66.

Assessments of the ecological tradition

Although Shaw and McKay's (1942) work on Chicago and other American cities has several facets, it is largely associated with the development of the ecological tradition within criminology. That tradition in turn was associated with the more general social ecology of Robert Park and his associates (1925), and suffered accordingly from the criticisms of the later 1930s and beyond. Although some have argued that all ecologists were tarred with the same brush (I. Taylor *et al.*, 1973), it is doubtful if Shaw and McKay relied greatly on the biotic model of ecology which was the subject of most severe criticism. As Alihan (1938), often cited as the main critic of social ecology, argued, Shaw interpreted delinquency primarily in terms of social, cultural and economic factors. He did not submit evidence to show that delinquency rates represented an *ecological* adaptation to different areas. Use of the concentric zonal model to describe areal patterns was clearly a borrowing from Burgess (1925) but this was essentially a descriptive device with no real theoretical implications. The theories which Shaw and McKay proposed, such as social disorganization, have been criticized but not because of any alignment with concepts such as symbiosis.

Partly because of some general association with a discredited theory and partly through dissatisfaction with its own more specific concepts and the scale of analysis at which it worked, the ecological tradition within criminology has diminished in significance since the 1940s. Mannheim (1965) for example, in his exhaustive review of criminological studies suggested that ecological theories had generally retreated into the background in the decades after 1945. Wootton (1959) suggested that ecological findings revealing that delinquency clusters occur in 'slummy' areas were of a mundane nature. More recent writers have echoed these views:

Ecology and epidemiology still exist in sociology, but as a source of ideas and commanding imagery, they have become almost mute. They tell us things, but intellectually they have nothing to say: they husband knowledge but not wisdom (Matza, 1969, p. 103).

This relegation of ecology may be particularly a feature of sociological studies and is certainly overstated in more general contexts. Baldwin (1975a) reviewed areal studies in British criminology and was able to identify at least twenty of these, half of which dated from the mid 1960s. A threefold typology of such studies stressed the continuing significance of research which established an areal framework as a means to an end:

> Ultimately, the detailed study of recorded crime in relation to hidden delinquency in selected areas, together with detailed studies of the local context and meaning of phenomena to the actors . . . should lead to gains in the understanding of selected types of criminal behaviour (Baldwin and Bottoms, 1976, p. 32).

This argument bears similarity to the grounded theory of Glaser and Strauss (1968) and the development of theory from empirical data. The 'means to an end' approach has already been used by geographers (Herbert, 1976) and will be discussed in a later chapter. For the remainder of this chapter the objective is to trace the modern form of research in areal and ecological traditions and its links with the emerging geography of crime. This discussion is organized into three sections. *Areal studies* focus on patterns of distribution, *ecological studies* on the correlates of crime rates at an aggregate scale, and the concept of *delinquency areas* allows the idea of specific territories within cities with high levels of criminality to be discussed.

AREAL STUDIES: PATTERNS OF CRIME

As geographers have become more directly involved in the study of crime and delinquency their analyses based on official statistics have focused on the depiction of patterns over space (Harries, 1974; Pyle, *ed.*, 1974). Involvement by geographers has meant use of a wider range of cartographic procedures including centrographic techniques and computer graphics, though the outcomes have been largely confirmatory of extant generalizations. Most analyses, however, have used general crime rates and there is considerable scope to discriminate between offenders and offences and among different types of offence. Schmid (1960) had already revealed some of the variability of patterns in his Seattle study. Pyle and his associates used a number of cartographic techniques to analyse crime distributions in Akron, Ohio, showing, for example, that violent crimes were reported mostly in the central city but that property crimes were dispersed. Corsi and Harvey (1975) depicted a number of crime 'surfaces' in Cleveland, Ohio, which contained the usual central city peak and localized nodes at regional shopping centres. Studies of this kind confirm zones and gradients and the earlier statement (Scott, 1972) that these had stood the test of time.

Despite this claim and the convincing North American evidence, recent British studies have begun to show sharp deviations from simple zonal patterns of crime rates. British cities have experienced significant restructuring as public sector intervention in the housing market has increased to levels of around 31 per cent of all residential properties. The new 'estates' located on urban peripheries rather than in the central city have involved the displacement of population from centre to periphery and the apparent transfer effect is evident in the geography of offenders. Morris (1957) studied offenders in Croydon and found that the clusters of delinquency residence, which tended to be small and localized, could not be generalized in zonal terms; the distribution could, however, be related to public sector

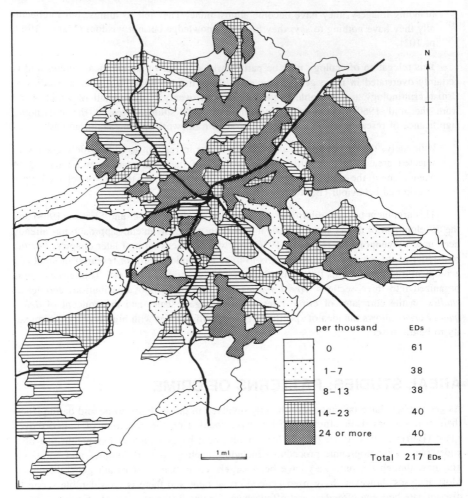

per thousand	EDs
0	61
1 – 7	38
8 – 13	38
14 – 23	40
24 or more	40
	Total 217 EDs

3.5 Offender rates in Sheffield, 1966. Rates of young male offenders (aged 10–19) by Enumeration District (ED). Source: Baldwin and Bottoms (1975) p. 76.

housing. Timms (1965) found central concentrations of offender residences in Luton but also noted peripheral high-rate clusters in interwar local authority estates. Baldwin and Bottoms (1976) found large central concentrations of offences in Sheffield, but offender clusters occured in inner-city areas, in housing adjacent to heavy industry and in some local authority estates (Fig. 3.5). For Hobart, Tasmania (Scott, 1965), a marked decline in central city delinquency rates and an increase in some suburbs between 1954 and 1961 was noted in relation to the development of government housing projects.

ECOLOGICAL STUDIES: CORRELATES OF CRIME

Ecological analyses which possess none of the symbiotic qualities of the earlier theory but which are distinguished by forms of procedure and scales of analysis, continue to be carried in a variety of urban contexts. Gittus and Stephens (1973) reworked Schmid's data on Seattle using canonical analysis rather than the factor analysis model. The advantage of canonical analysis is that it maintains the separation of crime variables and census variables and examines the relationships between the two sets. Despite the different approach the results confirmed Schmid's main finding with males and unemployed as the key census indicators linked with the crime dimension. Other more specific relationships could also be identified, however, with one link between Negroes and labourers and non-residential offences, and another between population mobility and cheque fraud and shop-lifting. Pyle (1974), also using canonical analysis, found a series of offence/environment relationships with an emphasis on opportunity structures. Corsi and Harvey (1975) measured seven crime variables against eighteen census variables, and their leading canonical variate suggested that rates of larcenies and car thefts were highest in areas occupied by professional people. This was interpreted as offenders moving into target areas, though for a second canonical variate which placed murder and assault in poor, substandard districts, a more 'local' relationship of offender and victim was envisaged.

Many recent studies have preferred to use a regression model to examine relationships, mainly because of greater ease of interpretation and more flexibility in a hypothesis-testing format. Y. Lee and Egan (1972) collected offence data in Denver, and by a regression procedure listed the main associated variables as distance from downtown, industrial activity and ethnicity; their explanation was couched in terms of lucrative targets and accessibility. Baldwin and Bottoms (1976) relied primarily on a regression model and used an input of thirty-one census variables, some of which were in composite form. Variation by type of tenure, labelled as a 'housing class' dimension, formed an important part of their findings. Socio-economic status proved a significant variable in local authority estates though much less so in owner-occupied areas. Social disorganization, measured as a composite of indices such as immigrants, small households and shared dwellings, proved significant in all private sector housing areas. The generally low offender rates in owner-occupied areas were explained in terms of policing patterns and the effect of property ownership on people's attitudes.

One variant of recent ecological crime studies is that which has attempted to link crime rates to typologies of residential areas. Polk (1957) initially found only moderate correlations between the Shevky-Bell constructs and delinquency rates but in a later study (Polk, 1967) was more supportive of the value of the typology. Willie (1967) used a modified version of social area analysis as a framework and found high correlations between delinquency and economic status (−0.64) and family status (+0.64) His conclusion that juvenile delinquency is associated with unstable family life and with poor economic circumstances has some credibility but tends to gloss over some of the relationships and caveats. More recently, Johnstone (1978) used social area analysis in a study of fourteen to eighteen-year-olds in Chicago and concluded that all forms of delinquency were related to what he termed 'social location'. Baldwin (1974) reviewed some of these studies and concluded with a preference for single diagnostic variables rather than social area frameworks.

There has in fact been a long-term search for single indicators in the criminological literature and the relative merits of these are now well researched. Some variables, such as unemployment and low income, have references going back to the middle of the nineteenth century as correlates of crime. Pyle (1974) in summarizing the most common single indicators, suggested a division into objective measures such as demographic, socio-economic, and living conditions and subjective measures, such as instability and stress. It is doubtful whether subjective measures exist in this single-stranded form but Fig. 3.6 summarizes some of the most common single objective indicators used.

Demographic features have consistently emerged as significant among offender

category	indicator	sub-group at risk

DEMOGRAPHIC
- age ⟶ young
- sex ⟶ male
- marital status ⟶ single
- ethnic status ⟶ minority group
- family status ⟶ broken home
- family size ⟶ large

SOCIO-ECONOMIC
- income ⟶ low
- occupation ⟶ unskilled
- employment ⟶ unemployed
- education ⟶ low attainment

LIVING CONDITIONS
- housing ⟶ substandard
- density ⟶ overcrowded
- tenure ⟶ rented
- permanence ⟶ low

3.6 Common objective attributes of known offenders.

groups. Most offenders are young; in the United States in 1971, for example, 52.9 per cent were under twenty-five years of age, with some variation by type of offence. In the same year 84.9 per cent of known offenders were male and females were typically shop-lifters or embezzlers. Marital status has often shown most offenders to be unmarried, though this may simply confirm the age factor, and children of large families and broken homes seem especially vulnerable. Socio-economic status has been suggested as a key indicator by several studies (Morris, 1957; Amir, 1971) which stress the large overrepresentation of working-class youth. Unemployment, in some ways a subset of social class, appears to have special significance. Ethnicity has been closely studied and the heavy involvement in crime of black Americans has been amply demonstrated; there was a United States black arrest rate in 1971 of 20.8 per 1000 against a white arrest rate of 4.5 per 1000. Again, there are several key intervening variables which need to be considered. Finally, adverse living conditions such as overcrowding and density are sometimes argued as independent variables though the case for substandardness *per se* is now abandoned with the experience of slum rehousing of the mid-twentieth century. Single indicators are attractive and can provide guidelines, but they need to be handled carefully in a statistical analysis which accounts for intervening variables and in a conceptual framework which retains awareness of the fallibilities of criminal statistics.

CRIME AND DELINQUENCY AREAS

The areal analyses which identify clusters of offenders in space and the ecological analyses which demonstrate their environmental correlates are brought together in the idea of crime and delinquency areas. Most references to such areas in the criminological literature refer to districts within cities which have disproportionate shares of both offences and offenders. The definition is stated in relative terms but the actual nature of such areas will be highly variable over place and time. Defined in these empirical terms, crime areas were identified in mid-nineteenth-century British cities (Tobias, 1976); in American cities in the early twentieth century (Shaw and McKay, 1942); and are observed in various forms in modern cities (Damer, 1974). Mack (1964) argued that although the mobility of the adult criminal makes the crime area a thing of the past, every large city contains delinquency areas characterized by exceptionally large numbers of young offenders. Such areas exist but are nothing like the equivalents of Merthyr's 'China' (Strange, 1980) or H. Mayhew's (1862) portrayal of London's rookeries, in which boys were born and bred to the business of crime.

Within the delinquency areas of modern cities, known offender rates never approach 100 per cent of the population at risk and rarely a simple majority. Edwards (1973) calculated prevalence rates for offences ever committed among a cohort of boys in Newcastle upon Tyne and found the highest ward rate to be 54.2 per cent. Forman (1963) and Kobrin (1951) found highest area rates of 20 per cent for court cases and 30 per cent for police contacts. In a detailed study of a British city, Mack (1964) discovered a criminal residence rate of 32 per cent in his worst street. Official data understate the rates and hidden delinquency is probably high in these areas, but the concept of delinquency area need not imply that all the at-risk population will become delinquent. Place of residence is but one frame of reference for adolescent behaviour. There are others such as family, school and teacher, workplace and interest group which may modify its effects. More narrowly it is argued:

> The reasons for not all working class children becoming delinquent may be listed as follows: (i) degree of stress resulting in psychiatric delinquency tends to vary with circumstances of individual families and personalities; (ii) not all delinquents . . . will commit acts which are specifically illegal; (iii) by no means all those who commit illegal acts will be detected and prosecuted and identified as delinquent within the definition of the law (Morris, 1957, p. 176).

Most modern descriptions of delinquency areas in the criminological literature have been conservative in their claims and have focused on their legibility within the city rather than upon any offender-producing roles which they might have. This is in contrast with nineteenth-century observers, who consistently proposed the 'breeding-ground' hypothesis (H. Mayhew, 1862). Shaw and McKay (1942) showed that delinquency areas could be identified, but stressed that the criteria used could not furnish explanations; these had to be sought in the field of more subtle human relationships and social values. Reservations of this kind are typical but more recent reviews continue to suggest that the significance of such areas cannot be overlooked:

> When we talk of a criminal area or of a delinquent sub-culture we are not saying that every individual living spatially close to the offenders is so powerfully conditioned by their attitudes and behaviour that he is obliged to break the law himself. What we are saying is that within a broad zone which can be drawn upon a map, a very substantial number of people commit offences and there is a general social tolerance extended towards this behaviour . . . the area as a whole is delinquency-producing . . . the exceptions do not disprove the generalization (Mays, 1963, p. 219).

From his extensive Merseyside studies, Mays was convinced of the existence of such areas and is concerned here to argue their reality; the phrase 'delinquency-producing' is used, however, and some causative element is clearly recognized. Whereas some criminologists (Mannheim, 1965) argue that subcultures have no necessary territorial base, much empirical evidence suggests that they do. Delinquency areas, once recognized, can be analysed in more detail. Shaw and his associates used such frameworks to examine the individual characteristics of offenders and to locate particular remedial schemes such as the Chicago Area Projects. More recent research has adopted similar attitudes and has proceeded from use of objective indicators to define areas with high offender rates and subsequently to the use of subjective data to investigate their character. Sprott (1972) suggested that once the incidence of crime had been plotted the climate of opinion in the streets could be studied. Morris (1957) was especially interested in proceeding to an analysis of the common social universe of which both offenders and non-offenders were members. More formally, Herbert and Evans (1974) proposed an area sampling framework from which comparative, qualitative analyses could proceed.

As a concept delinquency area has always proved difficult to handle and raises more questions than it answers. Some of these issues can be taken further in later chapters but it is pertinent to raise them at this point. How do delinquency areas arise and take on their characteristics? Does *area* in itself – as a surrogate for a social group sharing a common space – have some kind of independent effect which influences individual behaviour? The concentration of known offenders in a particular district of the city comes at the end of a long chain which links the allocation of power in society, through distribution of resources to its members, to the facts of unequal access to those resources in geographical space. At the end of this chain, delinquency areas are typically occupied by least advantaged sections of urban society and have also to be related to another 'chain' formed by the socio-legal system. This broader perspective is essential, but for theories such as social disorganization and subculture, which can be area-specific, and for geographers seeking to understand the differential response at individual and neighbourhood level to macro-conditions of disadvantage, delinquency area retains a role as a useful summarizing and investigative concept.

SOME GUIDELINES FROM AREAL AND ECOLOGICAL STUDIES

This chapter has reviewed the areal and ecological study traditions in criminology, traditions to which an emerging geographical perspective can most easily relate. The case studies which will be developed in the following chapters demonstrate this continuity, but some more general guidelines can be offered.

1. Non-geographers continue, both implicitly and explicitly, to recognize areal and ecological facets of their research (Baldwin, 1975a).
2. Most geographers studying crime are based in the United States and rather traditional areal and ecological approaches, based on official statistics, have tended to dominate their work.
3. The effects of more general methodological developments in human geography in the 1970s are becoming apparent in the works of some geographers on crime. Behavioural studies examining the spatial movements of offenders (Haring, 1972) and the perceptions of criminals (Carter, 1974) are examples of this trend.
4. There are useful developments which seek to link aggregate and individual scales of analysis (Herbert and Evans, 1974) and to focus on more subjective meanings of place

(Ley and Cybriwsky, 1974a). Here the established procedures of areal and ecological analysis may provide a useful framework.

5. More general awareness of the significance of socio-political processes and 'class conflicts' will lead to more research into levels of analysis which are antecedent to crime patterns as spatial outcomes, though very little research of this kind has so far been completed.

6. For the bulk of research which remains rooted at the local environment level significant roles exist. Separate strategies for analyses of offences and offenders are needed. Local environments as opportunity structures for crime, contain cues and stimuli to which potential offenders respond.

7. A geographical study of crime may well contain a prescriptive role and the scope for an applied dimension to research is considerable.

CHAPTER 4
PATTERNS OF OFFENCES: THE VULNERABLE ENVIRONMENTS

INTRODUCTION

The empirical study of crime is approaching its two hundredth year. One of the most interesting current thrusts in criminology returns us to concerns which marked the early phases of the systematic study of crime, namely the distribution of crime in space and what that implies for crime prevention (Brantingham and Brantingham, 1975, pp. 11–12).

Although concern with the incidence of offences rather than offenders and with crime prevention rather than crime causation can be traced to the origins of criminology, the 1970s has witnessed a resurgence of interest in these themes. Such an approach has distinct advantages. Firstly, broad contexts can still be recognized but active research may focus on narrower and more immediate factors related to criminal activity. Secondly, these factors involve analyses of the local environments within which offenders, police, and victims interact. Thirdly, the fallibilities of official statistics are reduced to the extent that much more is known about offences than offenders. Fourthly, the context of the local environment allows access to the roles of victims and their reactions to crime or fear of it. Lastly, such studies enable a much closer focus upon preventive strategies and on policies which may protect those who live in 'vulnerable' areas.

There are of course disadvantages to a focus on offences and local environments. Principal of these is the fact that such a focus takes no account of the recent methodological revolutions within both criminology and human geography. For example, it ignores the fundamental issues of class conflict and inequality which may provide root causes of crime, though there are links which need to be developed; understanding the incidence of some types of behaviour in space, for example, involves some comprehension of the way space is managed and how urban environments of particular quality emerge. Although the focus is on the local environment and what has been termed the third level of analysis (Fig. 2.1) these are not exclusive compartments and the interrelationships are always significant. The various levels are complementary rather than contradictory. For geographers interested in the analysis of crime, the emphasis on the 'situational contexts' of offence occurrence offers a field of research close to their most established range of expertise. This range extends from traditional techniques of land-use and morphological mapping to recent humanistic concerns with the subjective meanings of place.

The recent development of research interest in offence occurrence has two broad divisions. The first of these involves the attempt to distinguish *offences* and the ways in which *offence rates* are calculated as a separate field of study; the second centres on ways in which the local environment actually acts as a stimulus for criminal behaviour. Whereas the first of these is a pragmatic and technical issue which can be dealt with briefly, the second, with its far-reaching implications, has stimulated considerable debate and deserves close discussion.

OFFENCE – SPECIFIC RATES

Although criminological studies have long recognized the need to distinguish between patterns of offences and of offenders, the distinction has neither been consistently made nor maintained. Empirically there has often been some justification for this lack of distinction in the sense that offenders, particularly juveniles, tend to commit crimes in their own localities and the two distributions are coincident in space. This correspondence is variable, however, and conceptually is unsatisfactory in the sense that to the extent that offences and offenders relate to local environments, they relate to different facets. Offences, for example, may respond to opportunity structures in local environments, offenders to adverse residential circumstances. This statement needs qualification in detail but the main contention is that the relationships are different and that geographers and others need to study offences and offenders in separate terms. A related issue in the context of offence rates is the argument (Boggs, 1966) that such rates should be calculated against numbers of 'units' at risk rather than some general denominator such as area population. Shoplifting, for example, should be expressed as a ratio of number of shops or volume of retail sales and residential burglaries against numbers of residential properties. Baldwin and Bottoms (1976) adopted this principle to calculate an index of industrial and commercial premises in Sheffield against which to measure a range of offences against such property. Harries (1980) suggested that the general form for a 'risk-related' crime rate could be

$$Rrx = \left(\frac{\frac{Cx}{Rux}}{100\,000}\right)$$

where Rrx is the risk-related rate for crime type x, Cx is the frequency of crimes of this type, and Rux is the number of units at risk in a specific area. The logic of this type of argument is strong and such indices have been used to represent offence patterns in a more realistic form. Measurement is occasionally a problem. Risk units can be measured with relative ease for residential burglary, for example, but less so for offences such as cheque fraud.

DEFENSIBLE SPACE

Although some previous work can be identified, Oscar Newman's (1972) thesis of defensible space provides a useful benchmark from which the development of ideas on environmental influences on opportunities for crime can be traced. Newman himself is very careful to acknowledge the contribution of earlier writers such as Wood (1961), who produced a social theory on housing design, and Jacobs (1961) who was strongly aware of the influences of urban environments on social behaviour. A persistent theme in studies of this *genre* is that 'small is beautiful' and the dangers arise from the scale and speed of urbanization which may be such as to undermine the community bases of urban life. 'We are witnessing a break-down of the social mechanisms that once kept crime in check and gave direction and support to police activity. The small-town environments, rural or urban, which once framed and enforced their own moral codes, have virtually disappeared' (Newman, 1972, p. 1).

Newman's ideas have often been interpreted, rather mechanically, in terms of built environments and design; and although these were central features of his argument, the social interpretations of design are always implicit. This provides a bond with the recent work of social geographers (Buttimer, 1976) who focus very explicitly upon the human values attached to space and place. A general reaction can be identified in Newman's work against anonymity of segments of urban space and the creation of vacua within the social geography of the city. Such qualities may have been promoted by the design qualities of recent public housing projects in New York. Defensible space is proposed as the palliative to such trends and is defined in several ways:

1. as a model for residential environments which inhibit crime by creating the physical expression of a social fabric that defends itself;
2. as a surrogate term for the range of mechanisms – real and symbolic barriers, strongly defined areas of influence, and improved opportunities for surveillance – that combine to bring an environment under the control of its residents;
3. a living environment which can be employed by its inhabitants for the enhancement of their own lives, while providing security for their families, neighbours and friends.

Newman further suggested that there were four elements of physical design, acting individually and in concert, which contribute to the creation of secure environments:

1. territorial definitions of space by inhabitants;
2. an alignment of apartment windows which allows natural observation;
3. design features which avoid stigmatization (this element refers to public housing projects in particular);
4. location of new residential developments in 'safe' areas, i.e. low crime rates in adjacent blocks.

Whatever the merits of Newman's ideas, they have undoubtedly provided something of a catalyst effect in the field of crime prevention studies. Before looking at his own empirical evidence and at the criticisms of his theories, it can be noted that Newman was at least aware of the broader contexts within which crime should be considered:

> The root causes of inner city and ghetto crime lie deep in the social structure of our nation. Criminal and victim alike come from that state of population without the power of choice. In the United States, the correlation of criminal and victim with poverty is unmistakable (Newman, 1972, p. 13).

In the main defensible space study there was little more than an awareness of social factors. His focus was on the manipulation of buildings and spatial configurations and the 'permissive' influences, in interaction with social factors, which these might have. Table 4.1 summarizes some of the design characteristics which appear to reinforce criminal behaviour. Greater size and increased height of project were judged to be influential, though, as can be seen in Table 4.1(A), the evidence is not convincing. Highest crime rates are found in the large, high-rise projects but sample sizes are small. Similarly in Table 4.1(B), the category of project which has poor visibility (defined in terms of natural surveillance) has higher crime rates but entry definition (types of access) has little obvious effect. Newman suggested that many of the 'problem' projects in New York and also those of other cities, such as Pruitt-Igoe in St Louis, clearly lacked defensible space qualities in that, for example, they were stigmatized by their design features and were adjacent to districts of high crime rates.

Among the examples which Newman documented of defensive space qualities at work (or more typically *not* at work) were two projects of very similar size and social composi-

Table 4.1 Crime rates and urban design

A SIZE AND HEIGHT OF BUILDINGS

SIZE	BUILDING HEIGHT	
	6 storeys or less	7 storeys or more
Up to 1000 units	47 ($n = 8$)	51 ($n = 47$)
Over 1000 units	45 ($n = 11$)	67 ($n = 34$)

B VISIBILITY AND ACCESS

CATEGORY	CRIME RATE	
	Lobby	Elevator
Good visibility/good entry	7.3	3.8
Poor visibility/good entry	8.9	4.9
Good visibility/poor entry	7.2	4.1
Poor visibility/poor entry	8.6	4.6

Crime rates per 1 000 population; 'entries' are classified by the quality of their 'definition' in allowing surveillance.

Source: Data extracted from Newman (1972)

tion developed in adjacent areas of New York but at different times and with very different design principles. Brownsville, developed in 1947, covers 19.2 acres and contains twenty-seven buildings; Van Dyke, developed in 1955, covers 22.4 acres and contains twenty-three buildings (see Fig. 4.1). Both projects are composed of apartment blocks, but Van Dyke with a large number of thirteen to fourteen storey buildings is more typically high-rise than Brownsville in which three to six storeys is the norm. About 6000 persons are housed in each project, with similar densities of 288 persons per acre but the buildings in Brownsville cover 23 per cent of available land compared with 16.6 per cent in Van Dyke. Whereas the differences in design and sharply contrasted crime rates attracted Newman, he did seek to control social variables such as age, income, ethnicity, length of residence and domestic circumstances.

Forms of access were judged to be important. No Van Dyke building could be entered directly from the street; access was by paths, visibility was poor and entries served 112 to 136 families. Brownsville's more manageable 'zones' were more open to view and entry doors, with access directly from the street, served nine to thirteen families. Brownsville buildings possessed a sense of propriety with good mechanisms for supervision of children at play and general observability. Rates of tenant turnover were low, as were maintenance costs. Van Dyke was deficient on most of these characteristics and Newman argues that design differences between the two projects could underpin contrasts in crime rates and vandalism. For the rest of his book, Newman is concerned with elaboration, with examples, of his four principles of territoriality, natural surveillance, image and milieu, and with offering some initial design principles to achieve defensible space. There is strong advocacy for each of these principles but particularly perhaps for the development through design of opportunities for natural surveillance and the need to avoid established crime areas in the siting of projects.

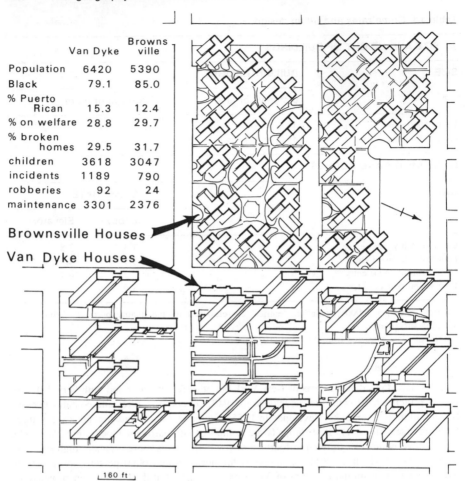

	Van Dyke	Browns ville
Population	6420	5390
Black	79.1	85.0
% Puerto Rican	15.3	12.4
% on welfare	28.8	29.7
% broken homes	29.5	31.7
children	3618	3047
incidents	1189	790
robberies	92	24
maintenance	3301	2376

Brownsville Houses

Van Dyke Houses

160 ft

4.1 Contrasted qualities of defensible space: the examples of the Brownsville and Van Dyke projects, New York. Source: Newman (1972) pp. 40 and 46.

Critiques and tests of defensible space ideas

Newman's ideas of defensible space have been controversial and have attracted a good deal of criticism (P. Mayhew, 1979). Most general criticisms have been of the methodology involved (Bottoms, 1974); the use of paired comparisons was very limited and insufficiently tested to give any firm bases for generalization. The examples quoted in the text provide statistics which are generally in the right direction to support the line of argument but are not always set in a rigorous research format; sample sizes are often too small to be subjected to tests of statistical significance. Hillier (1973) criticized Newman's (1972) use of territoriality as a concept and again the data in *Defensible Space* are insufficient to allow more than impressionistic judgements on the meanings of place. Newman's focus on physical design has made his thesis vulnerable to accusations of architectural determinism and although he was careful to control for social variables among his population groups and to acknowledge their roles, it was not until his later work (Newman, 1976) that he gave such factors more explicit and significant recognition. Without such qualifications his design concepts are extremely tenuous. Nevertheless the theory of defensible space certainly stimulated more research, some of which was specifically designed to test its principles.

Pablant and Baxter (1975) tested three main hypotheses in relation to the incidence of school vandalism. That low vandalism rates would be typical firstly, of schools with high aesthetic appeal and good maintenance; secondly, of those schools located in diverse and active neighbourhoods; and thirdly, of those with well surveilled sites. All these hypotheses correspond closely with Newman's ideas and were confirmed from the empirical evidence which Pablant and Baxter assembled. Leather and Matthews (1973) examined the local circumstances in which vandalism occurred and found similar support for some defensible space hypotheses. Both these studies were concerned with acts of vandalism or malicious damage, offences often unpremeditated or planned, and typically an aspect of adolescent behaviour. Research into residential crime has been less confirmatory of Newman's ideas.

Waller and Okihiro (1978) incorporated tests of defensible space ideas in their study of residential burglary in Toronto but found no clear evidence of their relevance. Repetto's (1974) study of Boston was based on data for 1988 residential burglaries and ninety-seven adjudicated burglars. Repetto's two sets of variables – social indicators and opportunity measures – involved a much more explicit use of social factors than those in Newman's original work. As Table 4.2(A) shows there were several significant sources of variation among the set of social indicators. A regression analysis showed ethnic composition of study area to be the most significant of these, followed by residential crime rate in adjacent districts. The set of opportunity measures gave Repetto his more explicit tests of defensible space ideas and included indices of visibility, design and social cohesion. Table 4.2(B) shows some of the more significant associations which emerged from this set of opportunity measures but over a number of elements which are central to the defensible space hypothesis, such as visibility and design of access and surveillance (admittedly posing serious measurement problems), no clear patterns of influence could be discerned. When analysis was narrowed to victimized dwellings, rather more support for design influences could be found. The probability of a dwelling unit being burgled was found to increase with the number of entry options available, especially in areas with high crime rates, and this was particularly true of small multi-unit dwellings. Additionally, quality of doors was a factor, and location of the dwelling at a corner appeared to increase its vulnerability (see Table 4.2(B)). Repetto's findings were more supportive of the influence on burglary rates of social factors, than of design principles. In his conclusions he was not dismissive of design factors – access and security were rated as key features of burglary-free areas – but his empirical evidence could not be taken as strong support for defensible space ideas.

Mawby (1977a) carried out a number of detailed empirical studies which were strongly critical of Newman's defensible space thesis. Part of the more broadly based Sheffield study, this analysis used data for four public sector housing projects which were labelled as council houses (CH) or council flats (CF) with high (H) or low (L) offender rates. When offence rates per 1000 residential population were calculated for each of these type areas, the scores of CHH 85.1, CHL 23.7, CFH 29.9, and CFL 20.2 were taken as contradictions of one of Newman's ideas in that low-rise housing had the highest offence rates. This in itself is not conclusive, as Newman stressed a combination of factors rather than height *per se*, and even on these figures offender rates appear more significant than height. More importantly, Mawby criticized the ambiguity in some of Newman's concepts. Although, for example, defensible space identifies design elements which may exert some influence on offence rates, the form of that influence may be variable. A garden for example, may present opportunities for theft but it may also provide a barrier between access road and dwelling; back windows can both increase vulnerable points of entry and allow

Table 4.2 Correlates of residential crime in Boston

A SOCIAL INDICATORS	ANNUAL BURGLARY RATE
GEOGRAPHICAL AREA	
Core	39
Adjacent to core	22
Outlying	12
ADJACENT AREA RATE*	
Low	8
Medium	28
High	55
RACIAL COMPOSITION**	
White	19
Mixed	40
Black	59
INCOME	
Low	47
Middle	27
High	13
PERCENTAGE OF PEOPLE	
Under 18 yrs	37
Age 20–29	18
Age 30–39	19
Over 40	41
HOUSE TYPE	
Single-family detached	14
Small multi-unit	30
Public housing	34
Large multi-unit	37
Large m/unit excl. lux.	57

B OPPORTUNITY MEASURES	ANNUAL BURGLARY RATE
SOCIAL COHESION	
Low	90
Medium	28
High	16
LEVEL OF OCCUPANCY	
Low	94
Medium	27
High	28
NUMBER OF DOORS IN MULTI-UNITS	
( ) LARGE M.U.	
One	63 (128)
Two	153 (86)
Three	474 (0)
CORNER LOCATIONS	
( ) NON-CORNER	
Single-family detached	253 (109)
Small multi-unit	194 (185)
Large multi-unit	273 (122)

Rates per 1000 dwelling units.
Last two sets of figures for victimized dwellings only.
Source: Data extracted from Repetto, (1974)
* Highest and ** second highest predictor variables from regression rates per 1000 dwelling units

greater observability. Physical design is always qualified by ways in which it is used and that usage will vary with the characteristics of offenders and victims. Mawby (1977b) also obtained data on vandalism for twenty-seven telephone kiosks in Sheffield. Visibility did emerge as a significant variable but had to be qualified in terms of levels of usage. Greater use of public space provides more observers and increases visibility but also provides more potential offenders. Kiosks in most exposed sites had high rates of vandalism but they were also the most extensively used.

A replicative study of telephone kiosks was provided by P. Mayhew *et al.* (1979). This Home Office study was more comprehensive and took as a measure of surveillance the number of domestic windows within a given radius overlooking the kiosk. Over a twelve-month period, the kiosks in the part of London investigated recorded an average of 4.7 incidents per kiosk compared with a national average of 2.2. The strongest observed corre-lates of vandalism were found to be the social characteristics of the residential areas in which kiosks were sited. There were correlations with density of population, with numbers of boys aged five to fourteen years, and with unemployment and low social class, but tenure was the most significant variable. Location in council housing estates was associated with a high incidence of vandalism. There was some 'window-effect' in that more over-looked kiosks were less offended against but social variables were more telling indicators.

Wilson (1978), in another Home Office Research Unit investigation, made an explicit test of some defensible space ideas. This study involved an examination of all public sector estates with over 100 dwelling-units in two inner London boroughs. Data were gathered for thirty-eight estates comprising 285 separate blocks which were classified as dwelling types into flats with gallery or balcony access, staircase access, or deck access, tower blocks, and row houses. Defensible space attributes which were measured included height and size of buildings, entrance features, levels of privacy, play facilities, and number of children. Individual blocks were scored for vandalism on a four-point scale. Location of recorded damage was: in dwellings 24 per cent, in lifts 26 per cent, in access areas 23 per cent, in communal facilities 12 per cent, in entrances 6 per cent, and 9 per cent elsewhere (grounds, garages, roofs). If lifts are excluded, 60 per cent of damage was concentrated on the ground floor and decreased steadily with height. A regression analysis showed child density to be the single most important factor in 'explaining' the amount of vandalism in each block and this was regarded as the principal finding. Wilson was not prepared to dismiss defensible space factors and argued that these should be incorporated into the future design of housing estates.

The question of surveillance, which was a central theme in *Defensible Space*, has received explicit attention in most subsequent research projects. As P. Mayhew (1979) argues, the police and other official security services have very little chance of actually seeing offences occur, so the public itself must fulfil much of the surveillance role. Experi-ence suggests, however, that the public will react positively only when there are factors which heighten their sense of involvement. Three 'groups' are most likely to pose a threat to offenders. Firstly, the police and security personnel professionally committed to defending property; secondly, neighbourhood residents with a sense of territoriality and propriety within their own district; thirdly, employees, such as office cleaners, who work in public places. How the surveillance potential of these groups can be improved is a policy issue which will be discussed in Chapter 6.

Defensible space ideas permeate the recent literature on crime prevention and have produced conflicting levels of support. P. Mayhew's (1979) conclusion that the thesis has considerable intuitive appeal but has been oversold is probably a fair assessment. Much of the 'overselling' arises from failures to incorporate, in an adequate way, the social factors which are only explicitly emphasized in Newman's (1976) later work. At that time he recognized the significance of factors such as proportions of families on welfare, in broken homes and the numbers of teenage children in a project or block. Other studies such as those of Repetto (1974) and Wilson (1978) confirm the importance of social factors. All these writers, including Newman, recognized that high socio-economic status apartment blocks suffered little vandalism or crime, whatever their design qualities. A range of factors from the 'quality' of the residents and their place in society, to their ability to organize security, affects the vulnerability of where they live; design elements are insufficient in themselves as sources of variation.

Some related strands from social geography

Some recent research in humanistic geography, although often not directed at problems of crime or vandalism, can be related to the debate on defensible space. Ley (1971), Buttimer (1976) and others are concerned with the human and social values attached to space and place within cities, and this research adds a significant dimension to concepts such as territoriality and community. Useful empirical examples of this type of research are provided by the studies of inner Philadelphia by Ley and Cybriwsky (1974a; b). One study involved mapping the distribution of stripped cars for part of the inner city; an offence involving both abandonment and subsequent vandalization and theft. When this distribution was examined in detail, it was found that the cars were clustered in areas which were interstitial to defined communities. They occupied the vacua in social space with little social control and sense of belonging. Similarly, an analysis of graffiti showed how these markings were used by teenage gangs to map out physical spaces or territories. Graffiti was used as a boundary marker and they concluded that the walls were much more than an attitudinal tabloid, they were a 'behavioural manifesto'. Buttimer sets this kind of empirical research in a more conceptual framework. For her, place and space are endowed with meanings by their occupants, space is 'pock-marked' with anchoring points of values, sentiments, and meanings. Theories of community (Bell and Newby, 1978) and neighbourhood (Sennett, 1973) can be interwoven with ideas of this kind to substantiate notions of place and territory in the study of vulnerable environments.

A similar approach to spatial patterns and interstitial areas is evident in studies by Brantingham and Brantingham (1975) of residential burglary. They developed the hypothesis that border blocks between established neighbourhoods or social areas are especially vulnerable to residential crime. Using data for Talahassee, they were able to show that border blocks recorded higher burglary rates than interior blocks and that the contrast increased towards the centre of a neighbourhood. The hypothesis here was that in such peripheral areas, offenders found greater anonymity arising from a less well defined sense of belonging and identity than would occur in the central core of a neighbourhood. Again, Winchester (1978) stresses the significance of population heterogeneity as a correlate of offence rates with the implication that less integrated space is more vulnerable.

Related research concerns the ways in which offenders actually behave in the commissioning of their offences and the general finding is that a majority only travel a short distance. This local nature of offending was confirmed by Baldwin and Bottoms (1976), who found little variation by social class or degree of recidivism, though older offenders tended to travel further. Haring (1972) summarized a series of American studies which showed some distance variations according to type of offence. For narcotics offences offenders had travelled an average of 2.17 miles, for petty larceny 1.83 miles, for burglary 0.77 miles and for vandalism 0.62 miles. Pyle et al. (1974) showed that whereas burglars travelled an average of 7.3 miles to high-income areas, they only moved 0.93 miles to low-income areas; violent offenders had typically travelled only short distances. Scarr (1972) and others have stressed the need to study the images of offenders and the factors they

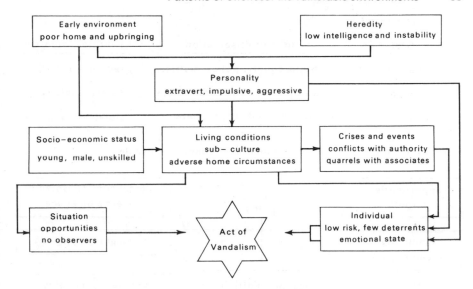

4.2 The background to an act of vandalism. Source: Clarke (1978) p.4.

consider in relation to opportunities for crime; Clarke (1978) offered a useful framework in which to conceptualize acts of vandalism (Fig. 4.2).

THE GEOGRAPHY OF OFFENCES: KEY QUESTIONS AND A RESEARCH FRAMEWORK

This review of the literature relating to offences, crime prevention and ideas of defensible space serves to identify some of the questions with which future research can be concerned. Firstly, can urban environments of particular vulnerability be identified and classified? Secondly, what key elements contribute to the vulnerability of urban environments to different types of offences? Thirdly, what is the balance between physical and social factors in endowing space with levels of vulnerability and how are these related? Fourthly, can the qualities of these areas be characterized in more *subjective* terms both by their occupants – the potential victims of crime for whom feelings of fear, safety, and security may be uppermost – and by the offenders, whose 'images' of these areas are critical to an understanding of their behaviour? These questions provide some guidelines which will be examined in a number of case studies; initially, however, a more general framework for such research is proposed.

Figure 4.3(A) summarizes the main scales of analysis with which geographies of crime have been concerned. The terms regional, urban, and individual are used to summarize the continuum from macro- to micro-scales of analysis. At the *regional* scale, a variety of observational units are used (see Chapter 1) including states and judicial districts in the United States and police force areas in the United Kingdom. The *urban* scale is centrally focused on variations of offence patterns within metropolitan or urbanized areas and aggregate units of observation include wards, census tracts, blocks and police patrol districts. At the *individual* scale the precise target for an offender, be it a person, a residential dwelling unit, a store or an alleyway, becomes the unit of observation. Whereas for regional and

A. Scales of analysis

Scale	Units of observation	Features studied
Regional	State; county; police district	regional variations
Urban	ward, tract, patrol area, block	spatial ecology
Individual	dwelling-unit, space, path	situational features

B. Variables in the offence environment at the individual scale

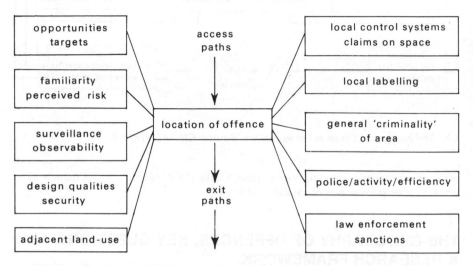

4.3 A framework for the geography of offences: (A) Scales of analysis; (B) Variables in the offence environment at the individual scale.

urban scales, the methodology of spatial ecology remains dominant, analysis at the individual scale invites new forms of investigation of the situational contexts in which offences occur. P. Mayhew (1979) identifies some of the factors involved:

> Stimulus conditions, including opportunity for action presented by the immediate environment are seen to provide, in a variety of ways, the inducements for criminality. These are modified by the perceived risks involved in committing a criminal act; the anticipated consequences of doing so; and – in a complex, interrelated way – the individual's past experience of stimulus conditions and of the rewards and costs involved (P. Mayhew *et al.*, 1976, pp. 2–3).

Figure 4.3(B) attempts to codify elements of the situational context within which offences occur. Offence location can be precisely identified and a set of environmental features related to that location can be measured. A comparative analysis may involve offence locations (based on official statistics) and non-offence locations, though identification of the latter is a research problem. Other elements related to offence locations in Fig. 4.3(B) can be contexted in ideas of defensible space, labelling theory, and recent work in social geography. *Opportunity* for an offence is a basic stimulus, and this is likely to be affected by the design qualities of the adjacent built environment. *Surveillance* is a significant aspect of design through qualities such as observability and nature of access. *Social* factors modify design qualities and physical space in many ways. Attitudes towards a dwelling in terms of security and behaviour in terms of frequency of occupance are critical. In the neighbourhood, the form of proprietary control over communal space and attitudes towards local environments outside the immediate dwelling are as significant.

Attributes of the situational context described so far can loosely be described as 'internal' to the locality, there are also 'external' attributes. An area acquires a *reputation* in part from the actual characteristics it possesses but also from the way in which it is viewed by outsiders. Residents of other parts of the city, official agencies and others may 'label' a particular area in ways which increase its vulnerability to crime. An area labelled unsafe or insecure, for example, could develop these characteristics over and above any internal propensity to do so. Adverse labelling of a residential area might lead to its avoidance by all except a particular category of occupants; the police could develop special attitudes towards such areas. Increased policing should deter offenders in some areas, but in others it may merely have the effect of increasing the amount of recorded crime.

A number of questions have been posed and a research framework has been suggested which is primarily directed at geographers studying offence patterns. Research by geographers however remains at an exploratory stage and the case studies which will be developed from the United Kingdom and the United States possess this quality. The South Wales examples will be developed with a research project (funded by the Social Science Research Council) in the early 1980s; Oklahoma City, which provides some comparative analysis, has already been the subject of a number of detailed studies. The focus in these examples will be on urban and individual scales of analysis.

BRITISH CASE STUDIES: A SWANSEA EXAMPLE

There have been very few detailed studies of offences at either urban or individual scales for British cities. The Sheffield project (Baldwin and Bottoms, 1976) collected data for 1966 in which 13 519 indictable (and similar) offences were recorded. This overall data set was sampled by various categories of offence to give a sample of 3444, and the distribution showed a heavy concentration in the city centre with 23.7 per cent within half a mile and 38 per cent within one mile. An index of industrial and commercial premises seemed to confirm the significance of opportunities but specific areas retained disproportionate shares of offences. Use of a rateable value index revealed the vulnerability of highest valued dwellings to house-breaking, but other categories of theft showed little correspondence with value of property. An example of violent offences did not confirm the previous finding of strong concentrations in particular areas (McClintock *et al.*, 1963); points of conflux such as bars and places of entertainment assumed importance in understanding the pattern. A summary of the Sheffield findings is that the city centre has far more offences than opportunity *per se* suggests and that recorded thefts from dwellings are not related to apparent rewards.

A set of data for Swansea in 1975 allows some offence patterns to be identified and discussed, and Fig. 4.4 provides some social geographical framework as context for these patterns. From this map the broad contrast between lower social status north and east and higher status west can be noted, together with the location of the larger public sector housing estates. Crimes of violence (Fig. 4.5) show a strong inner-city concentration which mainly reflects the location of places of entertainment. Dance halls, bars and clubs form the main points of conflux, and crimes such as assault are often associated with these activities. Clusters of offences outside the central area occur in a number of localities, principally one

4.4 Social class areas in Swansea, 1971.

of the 'problem' council estates. Sex offences cluster in parks, on open ground and other unsupervised recreational spaces. From this small sample, investigation has not proceeded beyond the stage of describing the distribution, but Murray and Boal (1979) have reviewed a number of British studies of crimes of violence. McClintock *et al.* (1963) analysed crimes of violence in London and found an inner city cluster; Lambert (1970) studied 562 disputes in Birmingham and found that whereas such disputes were comparatively rare, they arose mostly from domestic quarrels, street arguments or disturbances in public houses. Highest numbers of disputes were associated with landlord–tenant or tenant–tenant disagreements in privately rented housing. Disputes, it was argued, are symptomatic of the more general disorganization and instability typical of such areas.

There are many types of violent offence and McClintock *et al.* (1963) offered a condensed sixfold classification; the geography of violence tends to vary with type of offence. Much violence, as discussed earlier, is associated with social meeting places and is clus-

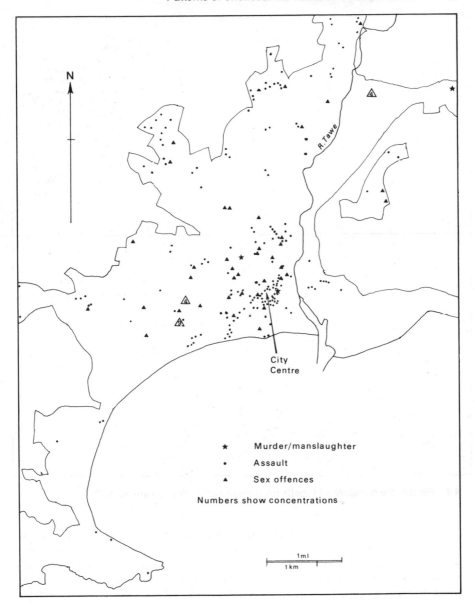

4.5 Violent offences in Swansea, 1975.

tered in entertainment districts; known domestic disputes are mainly found in low status residential areas. Evidence on association of violent offences with particular ethnic groups tends to be contradictory. McClintock thought that areas with Irish and West Indian immigrants in London had disproportionate shares of violent offences but Lambert (1970) found fewer offences of this kind in West Indian areas. Lambert's findings on private rented areas and the Swansea cluster in a public sector rented estate indicate some housing tenure context which is worth closer investigation.

4.6   Residential burglary and thefts from dwellings in West Swansea, 1975.

Residential crime offers more possibilities for research by British geographers both because statistical bases are larger and also because there is a more direct link with themes such as residential differentiation which occupied social geography in the 1960s and early 1970s. The concept of classifying residential areas can be developed into an approach which focuses on the definition of 'vulnerable' residential areas and for this the ideas associated with humanistic geography offer a valuable additional dimension. Figure 4.6 uses official statistics for 1975 and the street unit of observation to show the distribution of residential burglaries in part of West Swansea. There are distinctive clusters in this pattern but the correspondence is not with prime 'target' areas or the wealthier suburbs (see Fig. 4.4), even accounting for differences in overall residential density. A zone of high vulnerability to residential crime appears to run around the edge of the central commercial area and encompasses the older part of the inner city. At this scale the zones appear to comprise terraced-row houses in a variety of styles from simple workers' cottage rows to more substantial three and four storey dwellings, though variations within the zone are apparent. Within the zone there is mixture in terms of land-use and some heterogeneity of population, tenure and social class. Outside this inner city zone, clusters of residential crime are evident on some of the large public sector estates.

The inner zone of general vulnerability is further examined, though still in an exploratory way, by a number of steps designed to investigate variations within the area. Firstly, the scale of analysis is reduced from one of street units to one of individual dwellings; secondly, available small area statistics are used to context the offence patterns; thirdly, some survey procedures are used to test some defensible space qualities at this scale of analysis. The distribution of individual offences, burglary and theft from dwellings, confirms the strong variations within the inner zone. Although clear clusters of offences can be identified there are also segments which are free of offences. The plotting of evidence of acts of vandalism shows some conformity with residential crime but also reflects particular institutions such as the football ground.

Figure 4.7 focuses attention on one part of the inner zone in which offence patterns show strongest variation from one district to another. The selected transect can be subdivided into three sub-areas of distinguishable features, and these are marked on the map. The sub-area boundaries were selected to match census small areas but also correspond with known neighbourhoods in this part of the inner city. A set of draft planning cells constructed by Swansea Planning Department contains the three 'cells' of Sandfields, Brunswick, and Mt Pleasant, which closely correlate with the sub-areas, and among the natural communities named in the same document are those of Sandfields and Mt Pleasant. Area 1 (Sandfields) is virtually free of any offence, Area 2 (Brunswick) has a cluster of offences, mainly thefts rather than burglaries, and Area 3 (Mt Pleasant) has a particularly high incidence of residential burglary. The actual numbers of offences in each sub-area are shown on Figure 4.7(A).

Area 1 is a terraced-row district with a strong localized community ethos and a considerable amount of residential stability (Herbert, 1973). A number of local issues, including housing demolition schemes to accommodate road access and administrative buildings, but more consistently problems caused by football crowds and car-parking in narrow streets, have served to translate 'community' into 'communion' (Bell and Newby, 1978) and give the locality a sense of identity. On its eastern edge the area merges into the central commercial district and some intermixture of small businesses and corner shops remains typical of the area. Along Oystermouth Road a row of small hotels and boarding houses has developed in response to an emerging tourist trade. Area 2 (Brunswick) is distinguishable by greater land-use mixture and particularly by small businesses and commercial developments. Principal streets which tend to dominate the area are St. Helen's Road with its mainly retail character, and Walter Road which more typically has professional offices. Area 3 (Mt Pleasant) is sharply demarcated both by the main thoroughfare of Walter Road and by the topographical feature of the 'hill'. All its streets have access by steep gradients and are arranged along the contours of the southern slopes of Townhill. Above Mt Pleasant with its nineteenth-century terraces, often of three or four-storey houses, the large public sector estates of Townhill and Mayhill form a sharp contrast.

Figure 4.7(B) uses a small set of census indicators in order to identify some of the social characteristics which may underlie differences in offence patterns among the three areas. Census indicators are insensitive measures at this scale of analysis but can provide broad guidelines. Information on social class and car ownership shows general homogeneity over the three areas with some general tendency towards low socio-economic status. Census definitions of social class based on occupation tend to produce a large clustering into Social Class III, the intermediate group, but there are differences among the three areas in terms of the two extremes of the social class range. Area 1 is most dominated by lowest socio-economic groups with a ratio of high to low (Social Class I and II/IV and V) of 1:4.5. This

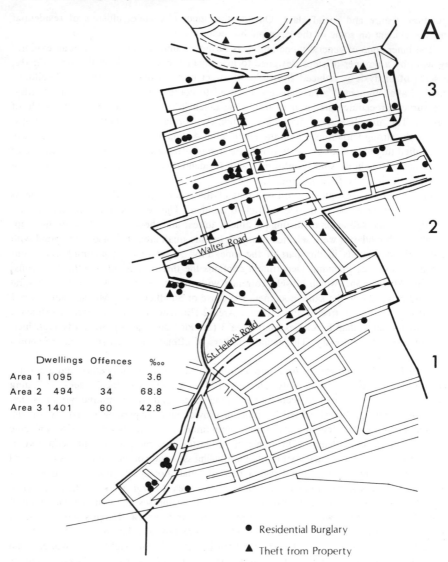

	Dwellings	Offences	‰
Area 1	1095	4	3.6
Area 2	494	34	68.8
Area 3	1401	60	42.8

● Residential Burglary

▲ Theft from Property

4.7 Residential burglary and thefts from property in a transect of Swansea's inner city area, 1975: (A) Offence patterns; (B) Social indicators.

compares with ratios of 1:6 in Area 2 and 2:6 in Area 3, which shows more heterogeneity in the last two areas. An earlier suggestion that Area 1 has greater residential stability is supported by the census indicator showing number of movers over the twelve-month period 1970 to 1971. Indicators on form of tenure support this portrayal of Area 1 as the most stable area. There are more private renters in both the other areas with two-thirds more in Area 2 and three times as many in Area 3. The indicator of shared dwellings shows a similar form of variation from one area to another. This set of census indicators offers some evidence which throws light upon the differences among the three areas and particularly upon the distinctive features of Area 1. From the offence patterns, Areas 2 and 3 are the

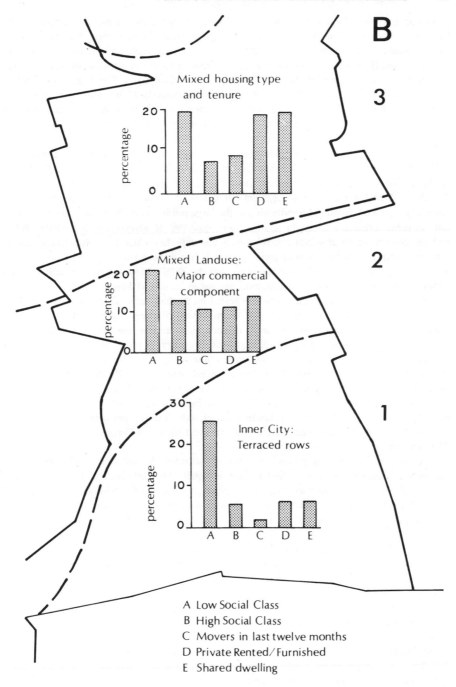

A Low Social Class
B High Social Class
C Movers in last twelve months
D Private Rented/Furnished
E Shared dwelling

most vulnerable and there is a consistent 'direction' among the indicators in depicting contributory underlying conditions. Winchester's (1978) suggestion that offences are more frequent in heterogeneous areas finds some support. Areas 2 and 3 with their higher levels of renters, shared dwellings and transients are more mixed in terms of population. Area 2 in particular has considerable heterogeneity of land-use with its shops, offices and small businesses interspersed with residential streets. Both Areas 2 and 3, though particulary the latter, contain streets or sections of streets in which high-income groups occupy enclaves in a predominantly lower socio-economic status environment. A process of social status change has affected parts of the area for a long period of time. The longest-established process has been one in which large row houses of formerly high status have been sub-divided and downgraded, but more recently evidence of some reversal of this trend is evident. Professional families, particularly at early stages of the life cycle, are moving into parts of the area and consolidating the enclaves of higher status.

Whereas the idea of greater heterogeneity in more vulnerable areas can be supported with some confidence, the other relevant hypothesis, Brantingham and Brantingham's (1975) of border zones, must be more carefully treated. To some extent it can be argued that Areas 2 and 3 are separate segments of a single 'border zone' between the stable, inner-city, terraced district of Sandfields and the large public sector housing estate on Town-hill. In these terms the areas do possess those qualities of anonymity, low observability and an absence of local social control which the hypothesis involves. Intuitively, there-fore, it is believed that the border zone hypothesis has some positive contribution to make in explaining the vulnerability of these areas, but the detailed investigation of attitudes and behaviour which would allow confirmation has yet to be undertaken.

Discussion of this example so far has rested on a small set of census indicators calcu-lated at an aggregate scale. On Fig. 4.7(A), however, offences are plotted by individual scale and some comments on the micro offence environment are possible. One striking feature of the distribution is that dwellings located on corner plots, that is on the ends of streets or adjacent to lanes, alleys, or some other form of open space, are particularly vulnerable to offences. Taking the eighty recorded offences in Mt Pleasant as a whole, comprising sixty-three burglaries and seventeen thefts from dwellings, twenty-five of these (32 per cent) were in corner locations. This varied from eleven out of sixteen burglaries (69 per cent) near Cwmdonkin Park, to fourteen out of sixty-four (22 per cent) in the rest of the area. Over the whole inner area, including the transect shown in Figure 4.7(B), the rate was 22.6 per cent.

A further, though still preliminary, investigation of the detailed individual offence pattern was undertaken as a student project in 1980. This involved a detailed land-use survey, information on the condition of properties, and signs of vandalism and insecurity. For each of 228 individual dwellings which were known locations of residential crime in 1975, a range of measures was recorded. In order to make comparisons with the offence locations, an equivalent number of dwellings with no recorded residential crime was also included in the sample. Selection of this latter set of locations and concept of comparison raised problems in the sense that burgled properties were selected from official data for 1975 and there was no guarantee that the offence-free locations had not in fact been the scenes of crime in 1974 or 1976. Again, official statistics were used and the incidence of unreported or non-recorded residential crime could not be accounted for. Other methods are available and will be used in the development of this particular project. A longer period, such as five years, could be used to confirm the absence of recorded offences in a particular set of dwellings or a victimization survey might be used for similar purposes.

Table 4.3 summarizes results for this comparative survey and focuses on differences between locations of known offences and those without recorded residential crime in 1975. The significance of corner locations is confirmed by characteristics of the offence sample; over half are within 25 yards of a corner and within 50 yards of a main road or open space. Figures for the control sample are not significantly different, though this is largely a function of selection procedures aimed at obtaining comparable locations. From the set of

Table 4.3 Attributes of burgled and non-burgled dwellings in Swansea

VARIABLES	BURGLED (%)		NON-BURGLED (%)		P =
LOCATIONAL					
Within 25 yards of corner	111	48.7	100	44.2	0.46
Within 50 yards of corner	97	45.5	88	43.1	0.36
Within 50 yards of o/space	89	52.9	71	46.1	0.54
SURVEILLANCE (EXTERNAL)					
Near street light	219	95.6	214	98.6	0.11
Adj. to vacant plot	25	10.9	13	6.0	0.09
Adj. to open space	31	13.9	17	7.9	0.06
Dense foliage adjacent	47	21.2	31	14.4	0.17
No facing window	77	33.6	64	29.5	0.40
No facing door	100	43.7	84	38.7	0.33
Over 100 vehicles/hr pass	86	38.1	69	31.8	0.14
Over 50 pedestrians/hr pass	103	45.0	102	47.0	0.91
SURVEILLANCE (INTERNAL)					
No back door	27	13.8	8	4.4	0.00*
No side door	42	18.5	24	11.3	0.05*
No back window	181	93.8	176	97.7	0.10
No side window	62	27.4	42	19.7	0.07
Front garden	155	67.7	143	65.9	0.76
Back garden	148	74.4	156	83.9	0.03*
Med./dense foliage	70	31.8	51	24.5	0.14
General observability	62	27.1	44	20.3	0.13
SECURITY OF DWELLING					
Open window	65	43.0	53	27.3	0.61
No security lock	141	84.4	129	80.6	0.45
Deteriorating frames	74	35.2	42	21.2	0.00*
Low general security	67	29.3	26	12.0	0.00*
SOCIAL FACTORS					
No sign of occupance	23	10.1	11	5.2	0.08
No one in at time of survey	77	42.3	81	45.8	0.58
Subdivided property	70	32.0	36	17.5	0.00*

* Significant at 5 per cent level.

Source: This set of data was collected by a group of students at University College of Swansea during February/March 1980 as part of a teaching project. The help of Dr Peter Atkins is acknowledged.

variables designed to measure surveillance, several show statistically significant differences between offence and non-offence samples. Offence locations have more side doors and side windows but fewer back doors or back gardens. A higher proportion of offence locations have medium to dense foliage in their gardens or in adjacent plots and gardens, and also tend to be adjacent to vacant plots or open space. Rather higher proportions, though not at statistically significant levels, have no facing doors or windows. A small set of variables was designed to measure security features of dwellings, though it must be noted that these were based on external observation of property only. Differences between the two samples were not statistically significant but rather more offence locations had no obvious security locks, had open windows at time of survey, had deteriorating window-frames, and showed no sign of occupance during mid-morning and afternoon. On a subjective five-point scaling of security qualities of the dwelling, a highly significant difference was noted between the two samples. Similarly, a 'social' measure, that of subdivision of dwelling, showed highly significant differences.

A number of contrasts between the two samples have been noted which can be rationalized into some consistent basis for comprehension. If analysis is limited to contrasts significant in statistical terms the pattern is less clear. Keeping in mind some of the precepts of the defensible space thesis, for example, significant differences between the samples in terms of observability and surveillance are evident. Any attempt to interpret the form of these differences, however, highlights some of the ambiguities of the thesis. For example, houses without back doors appear more vulnerable as do those without back gardens. On the one hand this could be taken as contradictory to defensible space ideas in that lack of access and lower surveillance might suggest less vulnerability, but on the other no back doors may be interpreted as greater security. At a liberal 10 per cent level of significance, more side windows typify offence locations which again could be interpreted as easier access (more vulnerable) or better surveillance (less vulnerable). A key statement here is that the significance and influence of design features, such as placement of windows and doors, must be interpreted with reference to ways in which those features are perceived and used by occupants and offenders. The variables which may be linked to this usage – amount of subdivision, signs of occupance, and overall assessment of security – all emerged as significant variables in the survey. The remaining significant differences relate to location near a vacancy or open space, a measure of surveillance and opportunity, and physical condition of window frames.

Overall, this reported study of a set of areas in Swansea provides useful pointers if not conclusive evidence. The suggestions are for support for concepts of heterogeneity and border zone location as correlates of offence-prone environments and a need to research the notion of community in place in a detailed way. There are design features of dwellings, detailed aspects of location, and form of adjacent land-use which appear relevant to concepts of vulnerability. These need to be considered however in close conjunction with a set of social measures concerned with attitudes, activities and broader questions of the values and meanings attached to space and place. Further research in Swansea will be developed along these lines.

AMERICAN CASE STUDIES: AN OKLAHOMA CITY EXAMPLE

There have been several significant studies of offence patterns at urban and individual scales, some of which have already been discussed (Repetto, 1974; Brantingham and Brantingham, 1975; Waller and Okihiro, 1978). These major studies have all been primarily concerned with residential crime and have produced useful hypotheses. The Brantinghams' borner-zone idea has been discussed, as have most of Repetto's main findings. Waller and Okihiro studied a range of socio-economic variables in addition to design features. Most of their findings are unexceptional. Victimized houses were less surveillable, adjacency to public housing increased vulnerability, as did low levels of daytime occupance. Studies of this kind provide valuable guidelines but the research priority appears to be one of bridging the gap between knowledge of the stimuli for offences which qualities of the built environment provide and an understanding of the social processes which give them meaning. This issue has not been fully researched but a number of studies of Oklahoma City can be used to exemplify the broad strategy for analysis.

A number of important analyses of the geography of urban crime have drawn examples from Oklahoma (Harries, 1974; Harries and Brunn, 1978; Carter, 1974). For the first part of

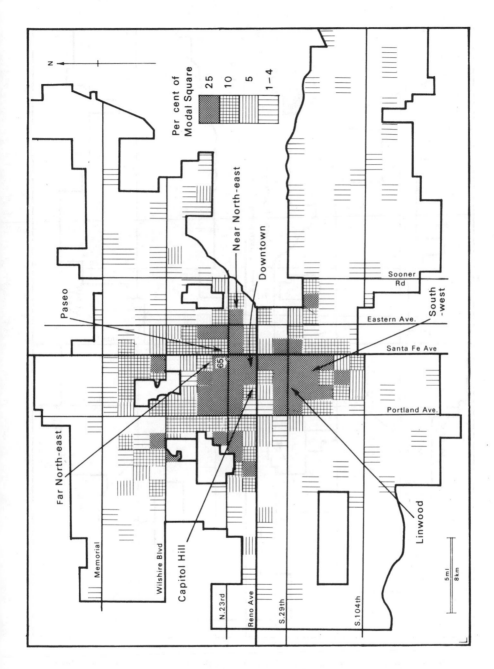

4.8 Robbery in Oklahoma City, 1978/79. Actual numbers are plotted by each square-mile grid cell over the twelve-month period: the modal square is indicated. Source: Information from the Oklahoma Police Crime Analysis Unit.

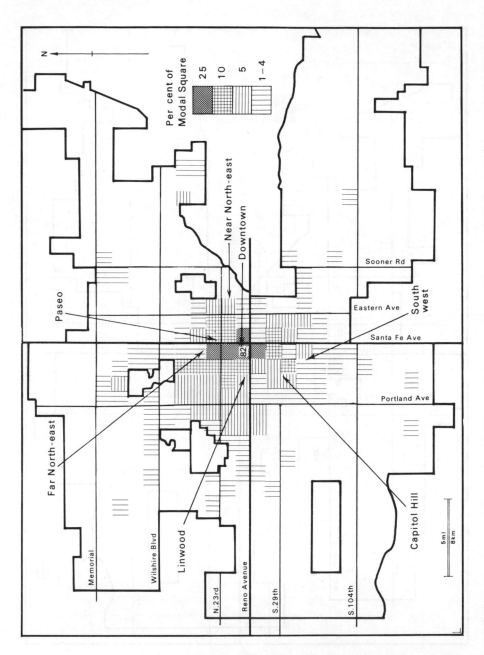

4.9 Residential burglary in Oklahoma City, 1978/79. Actual numbers by each square-mile grid cell are plotted for a sample of the first seven days of each month over the twelve-month period: the modal square is indicated. Source: Information from the Oklahoma Police Crime Analysis Unit.

this analysis, attention is focussed on two data sets, robberies and residential burglaries, collected for the period October 1978 to November 1979. Figure 4.8 shows the distribution of robberies against individuals for the Oklahoma police district, summarized into a square-mile grid. This provides an example of offences against persons and shows a strong central city concentration with very few robberies in the suburbs. This cluster is linked with transport termini, bars and other points of conflux in downtown proper, and there are extensions of high incidence rates east and north into high-density transient districts and ethnic areas. Paseo, one and a half miles north of downtown, is a deteriorating, former high-status area with a transient population; the Near North-east district is dominated by the black ghetto. There is also some lesser extension of high incidence of robbery west into the white, low-income district of Linwood.

Residential burglaries in Oklahoma City were studied over the same time period though only offences recorded in the first seven days of each month were included in order to retain a sample of manageable size. As Fig. 4.9 shows, the clustering of offences remains in the inner city, though outside the downtown area. Suburban rates of residential crime are generally lower than those of central city districts. The district extending northwards from downtown to Paseo with its subdivided dwellings and transient population contains one of the largest clusters, as does Near North-east with its black population and Capitol Hill south of downtown with its lower income white residents. Outside the inner city, there are less significant clusters of offences, some of which are associated with public sector housing projects occupied mainly by black tenants.

Figure 4.10 takes analysis of residential crime in Oklahoma City a stage further. One hypothesis from American literature (Repetto, 1974) is that black offenders are least likely to venture too far from their own neighbourhoods and certainly not into predominantly white areas where they will be conspicuous intruders. Similarly, white offenders are unlikely to move into black areas for similar reasons, but also because the likely rewards are small. Richer suburbs tend to be relatively offence-free, partly because of their security measures and also from their images as unknown and dangerous territories for the potential thief. Figure 4.10 identifies those offences involving black and white offenders respectively and shows their sharp spatial separation. Black offences occur in Near North-east and generally in the black ghetto areas. Other clusters of offences committed by blacks are found near public housing projects. Paseo with its transitional character contains greatest intermixing of offences by blacks and whites; elsewhere white offences are more widely dispersed in the city but rarely found in rich suburbs or in black areas. Another tested hypothesis was that older burglars would victimize more dispersed locations and more prosperous targets. The over-twenty-five-year-olds formed a minority group (about 30 per cent) and showed some differences from the younger offenders. Overall however these variations could not be generalized, and the hypothesis could not be supported.

Offence rates by square-mile units formed the bases of the distributions which have been discussed. As these units do not correspond with census tracts, interrelationships of burglary with social and demographic variables cannot easily be measured. At some stage in this project, when 1980 census data become available, such variable sets may be calculated. Some visual comparisons can be made however with two diagnostic variables mapped for different territorial bases within Oklahoma City. Figure 4.11(A) is based upon Polk survey data for 1977/78[1] and shows average household income by census tract. The accuracy of this data source in absolute terms is questionable but rather more confidence can be placed upon the relative differences which it identifies. The inner city emerges as uniformly

[1] Polk surveys are available for many American cities and are widely used for basic data bases during intercensal years.

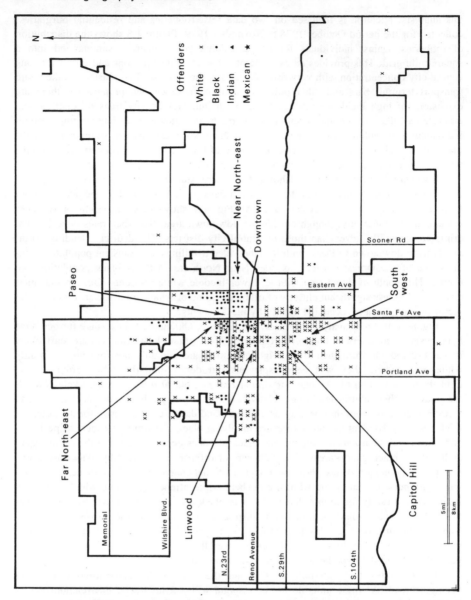

4.10 Residential burglary by ethnicity of known offenders in Oklahoma City, 1978/79. Information from that part of the burglary sample for which offenders are known. Source: Information from Oklahoma Police Crime Analysis Unit.

4.11 Social indicators in Oklahoma City, 1978/79: (A) Average household income by census tract; (B) Referendum turnout by precinct on state tax question. Source: Data from Polk surveys of Oklahoma City and Oklahoma County Electoral Board.

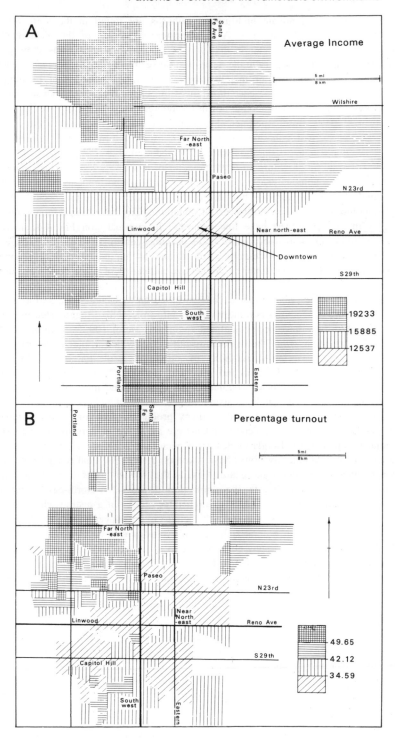

low-income and most dominant high-income suburbs are found in the north-west and south-west of the metropolitan area. A south-eastern extension of the black ghetto is reflected by the low-income sector in that part of the city. Income levels show gradual increases from centre to periphery in the north-eastern sector of the city but never reach the highest category. Comparison of this distribution of incomes with that of burglaries (Fig. 4.9) confirms the relative absence of offences in richer suburbs and a clustering in the generally low-income inner city though not in the poorest areas.

Figure 4.11(B) is more experimental and attempts to introduce a measure of neighbourhood awareness and cohesion. The variable used is turnout at a referendum in November 1979 on a state tax question which received a good deal of publicity. A working hypothesis would be that low turnout is an indicator of low awareness and lack of sense of belonging. This is a tenuous proposition and the results are not conclusive. High-offence areas do tend to have low turnouts but are not the only areas where this occurs. Offence-free high-income suburbs in the north-west of Oklahoma City have high turnouts, but similar suburbs in the south-west have low turnouts. In summary on Fig. 4.11 therefore, income as an indicator of socio-economic status provides confirmation of the characteristics of the offence patterns earlier described but turnout as an indicator of neighbourhood awareness provides ambiguous findings. Subjective indicators of place need more detailed investigation.

Offence patterns described so far have been based on the square-mile grid as a unit of observation. Figure 4.12 shows two individual square mile cells disaggregated into blocks for which burglary rates have been calculated against a base of 100 dwelling units.[2] There is considerable variation *within* the two square-mile units which in part represent land-use diversity but also the varying vulnerability of individual residential blocks. In Area 1, which is contained between Portland and May and 15th and 29th streets, a public sector housing project for a largely black population has been located in an area of low-middle income white housing. The public housing project itself, which is a mixture of small multi-units and row houses, itself displays many problems, with high vacancy rates and signs of vandalism in what superficially at least are attractive modern dwelling units with ample adjacent open space. Burglary rates are especially high in the adjacent streets of the white area, where individual dwellings have taken on a 'fortress' quality with high fences, iron-barred windows and doors and guard dogs. In the 'border' parts of this area, burglary rates reach over 30 per cent in a twelve-month period. Area 2 is North-east of downtown and has a more fragmented distribution of high rates blocks in a district where the black inner city extends into districts of marginally better circumstances. These two areas show how variability exists within general zones of vulnerability or risk. Particularly in Area 1, related qualities of social geography hold the key to an understanding of this variation.

Some final information on Oklahoma City can be drawn from a study by Carter (1974) which had the novel objective of seeking to understand ways in which offenders perceived opportunities for crime (mainly residential burglary) and acted accordingly. A sample of eighty-three offenders in custody was compared with one of seventy-nine non-offenders matched in terms of other characteristics. The offender sample contained thirty-eight blacks and fifty-two burglars. Information was gathered on where offences had been committed and also on fifteen areas which all respondents were asked to grade on a semantic differential scale for fifteen bipolar characteristics (see Fig. 4.13). Black and white offenders commit their crimes in different locations, with the former working only within short distances of the ghetto. The questionnaire study was comprehensive but a number of key summary

---

[2] I am grateful to Professor Keith D. Harries of Oklahoma State University for access to these data which formed part of an unpublished MS thesis by J. A. Sturdevant.

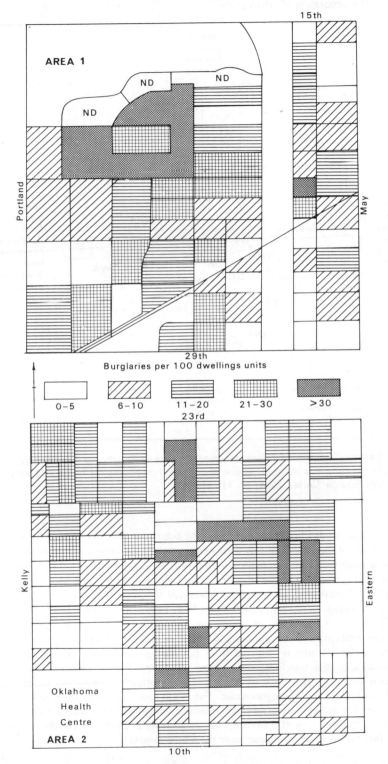

4.12 Residential burglary rates by blocks in two districts of Oklahoma City. Source: Sturdevant (1979) pp. 79 and 86.

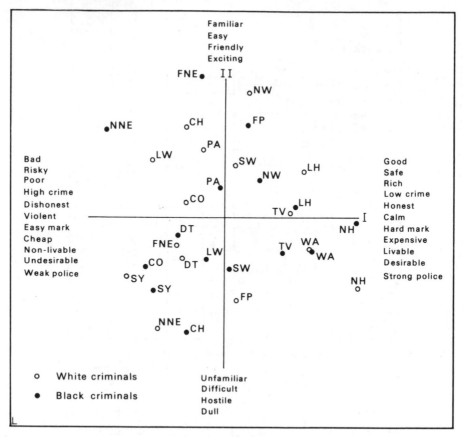

4.13 Offenders' images of fifteen residential areas in Oklahoma City. Diagrams show position of areas in factor space along two dimensions for black and white offenders. Source: Carter (1974) pp. 115 and 117.

statements may be distilled from it. Firstly, the behaviour pattern of criminals was related to their image of the city; criminals consistently stressed the importance of familiarity with an area, a quality of less significance to non-offenders. For black criminals, Near North-east was a discrete part of the city and dominated their perceptual space. It possessed familiarity and excitement and was highly favoured for crime. White criminals had a wider range of 'favoured' areas including Capitol Hill, Paseo, South-west and North-west. All offenders had a similar view of middle to high-income areas which they regarded as unfamiliar, hard 'marks' with too much security and police protection.

The further an area is removed from familiar ground, the more it is perceived to contain characteristics which discourage criminal activity. Figure 4.13 summarizes the different perceptions of areas held by black and white offenders along two factorial dimensions derived from the scaling exercise. Far North-east and Near North-east, which are rated as familiar and easy by blacks, are unfamiliar and difficult for whites; Capitol Hill and South-west are also viewed differently but in an inverse direction. On the axis of 'livability', there is greater concordance over the whole sample.

SUMMARY

From the empirical examples which have been described for Swansea and Oklahoma City it is clear that although good guidelines are appearing, research remains at an early stage. Available hypotheses involving physical aspects of design, land-use and location on the one hand and the 'social dynamic' of place and space on the other, have not been rigorously tested but deserve close examination. Theories relating to a border-zone vulnerability, heterogeneity and transience, and the general 'package' of defensible space ideas, are relevant to both the task of classifying areas of vulnerability and understanding the processes by which offenders, victims, and agents of control interact. A conceptual framework within which this variety of approaches can be contained has been proposed (Fig. 4.3) and the need to doubt the independent significance of individual measures of local environment has been stressed. Taken together these individual measures assume meaning and here may lie the potential of a social geographical approach to the study of offence patterns. Such a perspective should construct the socio-spatial context for features of design and the built environment, place 'borders' in social geographical space, interpret heterogeneity in its territorial meaning, and encompass the subjective values attached to place and space. These are some of the lines along which a geography of offences can be developed.

CHAPTER 5
WHERE OFFENDERS LIVE: THE PROBLEM AREAS

INTRODUCTION

Ecological studies of offenders have mainly been concerned with their distribution in social and geographical space and with their correlates in the urban environment. This emphasis has not been significant in criminology as a whole, and even for Shaw and McKay, who made major contributions to the ecological tradition, it was not always the dominant theme in their work. During the 1970s geographers studying crime found most common ground with the methodology of ecologists, but there was a growing awareness that the depiction of patterns of offenders and the measurement of correlations were insufficient bases for research. As earlier ecologists were drawn towards sociological theories to explain the patterns which they observed, and rightly viewed these patterns as merely spatial outcomes of some more general malaise, so geographers need to view spatial ecology and area analyses in similar limited ways.

These research traditions, of which ecology formed a part, have tended to remain bedded in the context of localized groups and environments and became the object of considerable criticism from deviance theorists in the early 1970s. Phillipson (1971) suggested that studies of offenders which seek to examine causation have a long history of failure; the need now is to look for root causes in the organization of society and the nature of class conflicts. This debate is discussed in Chapter 2 and need not be repeated here, though its relevance to recent empirical work remains considerable. In the course of this chapter a number of case studies will be introduced which do not attempt to add to the 'history of failure' in seeking the causation of crime but have the more limited goal of seeking to understand why known offenders are clustered in particular areas in cities and what features these areas possess. Traditional procedures of depicting patterns of offenders and measuring the correlates of offender rates form part of the case studies, but from these are developed analyses of the subjective qualities of delinquency areas and of their emergence and persistence. This analytical strategy focuses on the third level of analysis described in Chapter 2 and the local environments in which offenders live. For some of the themes, particularly that of the emergence of problem areas, the second level of the urban managers becomes relevant and, generally, an awareness of the broader contexts is essential. The justification for this kind of analysis, as argued earlier, is that however deeply rooted in the inequalities of the system the origins of crime lie, they produce a variable response. The radical critique has sharpened our awareness of the contextual frameworks within which offenders are defined and identified; it has done little to explain the considerable variability in social behaviour which emerges from those contexts.

Baldwin (1975a) provided a useful review of the areal and ecological traditions in British criminology in which he was able to identify a significant number of recent or ongoing studies. He found several weaknesses in this type of approach. Firstly, he argues, all such studies tend to be based upon official measures of criminality ; secondly, the common reliance on small area statistics raises the caveat of ecological fallacy. Baldwin suggests three types of areal analysis, a term used in preference to ecological analysis with its symbiotic connotations, in British criminology: (1) studies in which areal analysis emerges as a byproduct of other concerns; (2) studies in which areal analysis is an end in itself; (3) studies in which such analysis is used as means to an end. Of these the second has value as a portrayal of problems and an inventory of the incidence of offenders, but the last has most potential value. There are precedents in the literature for the use of area analysis as a means to an end. Morris (1957) proceeded from such analysis to a discussion of the segregation processes which led to the emergence of problem areas; Sainsbury (1955) integrated aggregate analyses with individual case studies in his investigation of suicide in London; and Jephcott and Carter (1954) followed an identification of problem streets in Nottingham with an examination of the 'climate of opinion' within them. The case studies which will be discussed build on these ideas.

Most of these case studies are based on the city of Cardiff which is the largest city in Wales with a population of just under 300 000. A number of research projects have been completed, the largest of which was funded in part by the Home Office Research Unit over the period 1972 to 1973. Data sources for these projects comprise official statistics on juvenile offenders for two years, 1966 and 1971. These statistics were mainly obtained from the police department under appropriate conditions of confidentiality and were supplemented by information from welfare services in the city. The particular years were chosen to coincide with census dates, and offender rates calculated for enumeration districts could be related to a wide range of census variables. Small area boundaries were not constant over the five-year period and for one stage of analysis, the 1971 data, both delinquency and census variables were recalculated to 1966 small areas to aid comparability. Qualitative data were obtained from a questionnaire survey of 500 households divided among six residential areas in the city. Reporting of results from these projects is organized in a number of stages: (1) areal patterns are described; (2) ecological associations are related to a small number of research hypotheses; (3) an area sampling framework is devised to study the subjective environments; (4) some issues on the emergence of problem areas are discussed.

OFFENDER PATTERNS IN CARDIFF

Several studies (Herbert, 1970; Evans, 1973) have examined the general social geography of Cardiff and some brief notes serve as a backcloth to the study of delinquency. The city grew as a major port and commercial centre in the late nineteenth and twentieth centuries serving a rapidly expanding hinterland in industrial South Wales. Although the port function has diminished and the fortunes of the hinterland have declined in recent years, Cardiff has continued to grow as a service centre and has assumed an increasing number of roles in association with its position as capital city of Wales. The city is large enough to display a distinctive and diverse residential mosaic, and the dockland district, although affected by renewal, still houses a largely residual immigrant community. Around the city centre are the closely built-up workers' terraces of the nineteenth century which have been variously affected by urban renewal and clearance schemes. Some inner-city districts of larger houses have been downgraded with subdivision and tenancy by transient populations, but in a sector extending northwards through Cyncoed, higher status residences persist. Modern private housing occurs on the city periphery though there has been a significant expansion into semi-rural areas outside the city limits. Public sector housing has made a considerable impact on the social geography of the city with small projects, including high-rise apartments, in the inner city and large estates on the periphery. The city of Cardiff provides a diverse urban setting about which a great deal of detailed knowledge has been accumulated; its crime rates were well above average (see Chapter 1) and it forms an eminently suitable study area.

The two main data sets on offenders included all juveniles aged ten to nineteen known to the police and receiving some kind of official sanction in 1966 or 1971. The age nineteen years was used as a threshold rather than the official delinquency threshold of seventeen years in order to increase sample size. Samples were obtained of 718 in 1966 and 914 in 1971; a correlation test of the ten to nineteen with the ten to seventeen group showed no significant difference and the data set was taken as representative of officially defined delinquents. Enumeration districts were used as units of observation and sixteen delinquency rates were calculated for each year against the appropriate populations at risk. Table 5.1 summarizes some characteristics of each group of offenders. Males outnumber females on a 4:1 ratio and most offenders come from older age groups. Between 35 and 40 per cent of

Table 5.1 Composition of the delinquent groups: Cardiff, 1966 and 1971

	1966	1971
SEX DISTRIBUTION		
Male	80	79
Female	20	21
AGE DISTRIBUTION		
10–11		5.6
12–13		16.7
14–15		26.6
16–17		24.2
18–19		26.9
FAMILY SIZES		
1–4	29.9	23.6
5–6	33.4	36.5
7 or more	36.6	39.9
NO. OF ASSOCIATES IN OFFENCE		
0	35.1	47.2
1	28.1	24.8
2	14.8	11.3
3	8.4	8.7
4–6	11.1	4.5
7 or more	2.5	3.5
OCCUPATIONAL STATUS OF HEAD OF HOUSEHOLD		
Professional/managerial	1.9	1.8
Other non-manual	10.7	8.0
Supervisory	3.3	1.2
Skilled manual	57.0	53.5
Semi-skilled manual	3.0	6.7
Unskilled manual	8.8	4.9
Self employed	10.4	10.4
Unemployed	4.9	13.5

All figures are percentages

offenders come from families with seven or more members; for Cardiff as a whole only 7.6 per cent of households have six or more members. Most offenders committed their delinquent act with one or more associates and about two-thirds came from homes of manual workers. Of those offenders in 1966 for whom information was available, 22 per cent were

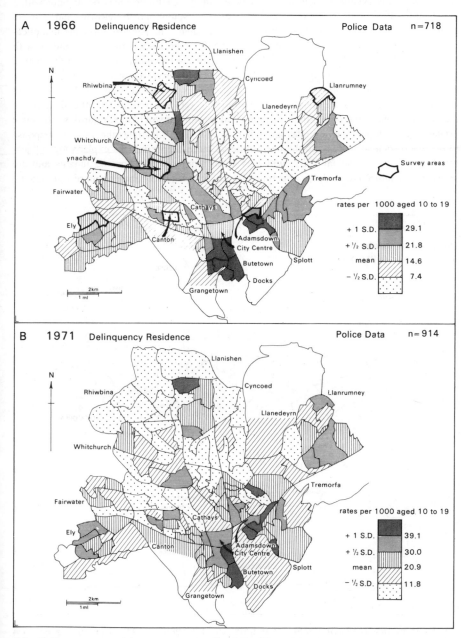

5.1   Delinquency residence rates in Cardiff: (A) 1966, showing areas selected for detailed study; (B) 1971. Source: Herbert (1976) pp. 478 and 479.

unemployed and in both years around 15 per cent came from broken homes. These are known offenders and their characteristics conform with expectations from previous litera-ture.

Figure 5.1 shows the spatial distribution of all juvenile offenders in 1966 and 1971 and also shows areas eventually selected for detailed study. High-rate areas occur both within the central city, in districts such as Adamsdown, Splott and Butetown, and also in peripheral estates such as Ely, Llanrumney and Llanishen. The patterns show the inapplica-bility of simple centre–periphery hypotheses, confirm the associations of offenders with some public housing estates, and provide evidence of the variablity both within the central city and among public housing estates. This last point deserves emphasis. Using objective measures, much of the inner city could be classified as low social status and substandard housing, but some parts are clearly more 'delinquent' (at least in terms of official statistics) than others. Again, the populations of municipal housing have broad similarities, but some estates have high delinquency rates and others do not. This illustrates the variable response to the macrosocietal forces and the need to delve more deeply into its explanation. Objec-tive factors, such as social class, will vary even among public housing tenants and are relevant, but subjective qualities affecting attitudes and behaviour may be more significant.

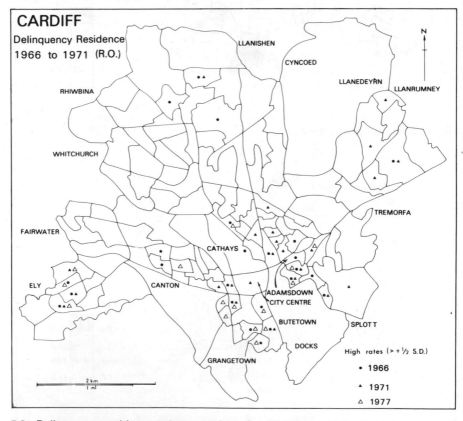

5.2 Delinquency residence rates over time, Cardiff 1966 to 1977. For 1977 areas are marked where rates are more than one standard deviation above the mean. Source: Herbert (1977) pp. 88 and Evans (1978) p. 39.

The years 1966 and 1971 provide 'snapshots' of patterns at two points in time, but some discussion of change is possible. There is in fact a considerable amount of stability in offender patterns over the two years and a coefficient of +0.43, significant at the 0.01 per cent level, confirms this. Some changes can be identified and generally these either reflect an estate's youth population progressing through the life cycle or indicate the effects of population transfer from inner city to peripheral estate. Delinquents in the older (fifteen to nineteen years) end of the age-band are more common in older estates such as Ely and Rumney, younger delinquents (ten to fourteen years) typify newer estates such as Llanedeyrn. Figure 5.2 shows high-rate areas for more serious offenders (using police department RO classifications) which are concentrated in the inner city in 1966 but have to some extent dispersed outwards by 1971. Some measure of further change is given by indicators from an analysis of 783 juvenile offenders in 1977 from Social Services department records (Evans, 1978). These show clusters in the inner city and on the Ely estate, but all other public housing estates have below average offender rates. Too much cannot be inferred from one data set but there is some suggestion of socialization over time. Delinquent behaviour may be 'transferred' to new homes but can modify over time except where an estate is adversely labelled. This proposition is not substantiated but may be worthy of further research.

Most areal analyses have been confined to aggregate statistics but for the Cardiff data sets it was possible to examine patterns at an individual level. Graphical presentation is designed to prevent precise identification of offenders' addresses but nevertheless allows the essential features to be discerned. Figure 5.3 shows a section of the eastern side of the inner city in which the individual residences of offenders are indicated. Several clusters are apparent and several households contain more than one offender. The pattern has to be treated with caution in the sense that it records only known offenders in one year and also because the distribution of all juveniles aged ten to nineteen is not known at this scale. It does provides tentative evidence for 'black' and 'white' streets (Morris, 1957) within a problem area. The analysis can be taken one stage further by identifying some of the links among offenders. Almost half of the offenders were apprehended with others (as recording practice is variable this is probable an underestimate) and it is possible to construct some of these connections (see inset to Fig. 5.3). Within this subgroup of eleven offenders, all were interlinked directly or indirectly in the commissioning of seven offences. This particular network is certainly not complete as for the same seven offences ten other offenders were recorded, but as either names or addresses were not noted, they could not be located in the diagram. This is a delinquent network based on a residential district but also involving other meeting places, such as school or club; there was a strong age-banding among associates in any one offence.

Similiar exercises with individual addresses were completed for two estates. Again clusters in particular streets could be identified and some links among offenders could be constructed (see Herbert, 1979b). Spatial contiguity within residential districts is clearly of limited significance in explaining groups of offenders at this scale of analysis. A specific test of distance effects involved use of a grouping technique to reduce 157 individual observations ot fifty spatial clusters and a comparison of these with known linkages. The two groupings did not correspond and a simple distance hypothesis is not tenable; spatial analysis of patterns needs to be allied to direct surveys of the offenders. For the youth on an estate, residence is but one spatial reference point. Other meeting places are strongly relevant to patterns of human association and non-spatial factors are obviously relevant. Clusters occur within problem areas but do not always represent active delinquent groups. It is residence *within* the estate which is relevant and the implications which this has for shared values and standards and also for common facilities and institutions. Spatial relationships

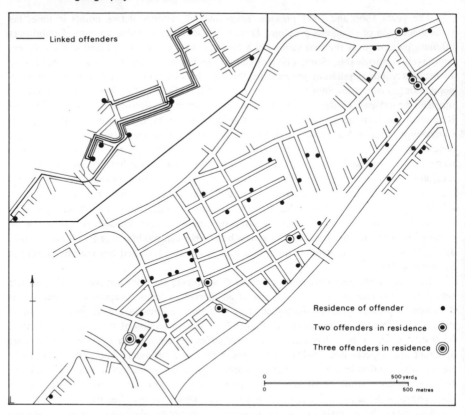

5.3 Residences of individual offenders in an area of Cardiff, inset shows actual links among offenders. Data for juveniles in 1971. Source: Herbert (1977) p. 90.

and distance separation, aspects of the 'geometry of space', have little meaning unless they are viewed in terms of a social context in which the relevant values and meanings are introduced.

ECOLOGICAL ASSOCIATIONS

Spatial ecologies of crime and delinquency data have consistently tried to identify key correlates of offender rates and to use these as bases of explanation. This type of exercise is very vulnerable to over-ambitious interpretations of statistical association of which the recent study of a town in northern England (Brown *et al.*, 1972) provides an example. Among the theories for which they claimed to have found support were anomie, subculture, retreatism and double-failure. Hirschi and Selvin's (1967) early plea for procedural rigour and for circumspection in inferences drawn from this type of analysis deserves close attention. Their other suggestion, that circumspection might be achieved by placing less emphasis on the identification of causes and more on understanding the general conditions under which criminal and delinquent behaviour is precipitated, should serve as a general guideline. For purposes of this discussion, three types of hypothesis relevant to the ecological tradition will be discussed with empirical examples. The first of these covers a group of theories, such as social disorganization and anomie, which date from ecology of the 1920s and 1930s; secondly a set of less theory-based hypotheses which describe the clustering of 'malaise' indicators of which crime is one facet; and thirdly, a more recent hypothesis which is not adequately theorized but does offer a link between manifest problems and the allocation of resources in competitive markets will be discussed.

Hypothesis type 1: Correlations and traditional theories

Several major theories seek to relate the high incidence of offenders in particular groups and areas to some underlying social condition which is essentially local in its effects. Shaw and McKay's (1942) use of social disorganization theory was typical of this suggestion. High delinquency rates, population turnover, families on welfare and other variables were regarded as symptomatic of a disorganized condition. Mays (1963) was one critic of this theory and argued that criminals were found in areas where social order was the norm. Baldwin and Bottoms (1976) used a composite measure of social disorganization in their Sheffield study and found it to have diagnostic value in privately owned sectors of housing. Lander (1954) used correlation and regression techniques to analyse associations between delinquency and social variables in Baltimore and found support for the concept of anomie.

There is a considerable list of research investigations of this kind which use evidence from statistical relationships to support theories relating to local social conditions. These have primarily used objective indices and many have read too much causality into correlations. It is worth remembering that Clifford Shaw, who was always extremely careful in his claim for ecological analysis, both identified the origins of crime in the 'deeper roots' of society and also augmented his aggregate analyses of crime data with detailed case histories of individual offenders incorporating essentially qualitative and subjective information. The study of the jack-roller (Shaw, 1930) is probably the best-known of these case histories and, of other Chicago contemporaries, Thrasher's (1927) classic study of teenage gangs followed an anthropological style of research. Even when ecological approaches were used as bases for theories, therefore, these were often linked with other kinds of analysis and studies of subjective environments have increasingly been incorporated as the shift to sub-cultural theories has gathered force.

Hypothesis 2: Descriptive statistics and the poor environment concept

The second set of hypotheses is less explicitly tied to any more general theory but has the broad aim of describing the group of indicators with which crime and delinquency are associated. In general these can be summarized as 'poor environment' hypotheses identified by a set of indicators which in various ways suggest adverse living conditions and socio-economic circumstances. Earlier emphases on the physical conditions of life became muted in the twentieth century as the advent of better housing failed to lead to significant decreases in numbers of offenders. Slum clearance schemes appeared to have the effect of displacing rather than diminishing high levels of delinquency, and Michelson (1970) argues that only in extreme conditions are physical environments *per se* likely to 'produce' offenders. The most relevant indicators are now found in the social rather than the built environment

Data from the Cardiff study can be used to demonstrate the persistence of the poor environment hypothesis. Table 5.2 shows the two sets of variables, delinquency and census, which formed inputs for the correlative exercises. The delinquency variables are all measures of delinquency residence (homes of known offenders) and distinguish offender rates according to the seriousness of the offence, sex, age group, type of offence and punishment. Census variables were selected with reference to available literature and cover a range of social, economic, and demographic characteristics. Previous applications of

Table 5.2 Variables used in the Cardiff study

DELINQUENCY VARIABLES	CENSUS VARIABLES
1. All offenders	Sex ratio
2. More serious offences	Aged 0–19 years
3. Less serious offences	Foreign born
4. Male offenders	Sharing dwelling
5. Female offenders	Without exclusive use of all amenities
6. Offenders aged 10–14 years	Owner occupiers
7. Offenders aged 15–19 years	Local authority tenants
8. Offences against persons	Private tenants
9. Offences against property	Movers within the local authority (1961–66)
10. Larceny offences	Movers into the local authority (1961–66)
11. Offenders cautioned or	Social Classes 1 and 2
conditionally discharged	
12. Offenders fined ·	Social Classes 4 and 5
13. Offenders placed on probation	Unemployed males
14. Offenders placed in care	Households with 5 or more persons
15. Male offenders aged 15–19 years	Households at over 1.5 persons per room
16. Offenders aged 10–17 years	Households without fixed baths
17.	With Ordinary National or Advanced level
18.	Lone parent households

All delinquency variables were calculated as rates per 1 000 population at risk; all census variables, except No. 1, were calculated as percentages. Sex ratio was expressed as females per 100 males. All variables were calculated for the areal units formed by the 1966 enumeration districts for both 1966 and 1971. Census variables 17 and 18 were only available for 1971 and were only used in the regression analysis.

factor analysis to data sets of this kind (Schmid, 1960) have included crime and census measures in single inputs. These procedures have linked high offender rates with measures of a poor environment and tend to confirm the general hypothesis. They have been criticized, however, on the grounds that the overall effect will be to identify only a broad relationship and to crystallize the two data sets as separate factors. This indeed proved to be the case with the Cardiff data, where taking a set of factorial solutions, from primary to promax oblique, the overriding tendency was for the delinquency and census sets of variables to be separately associated with almost discrete factors. Only in the leading primary factor, which had high loadings with most of the delinquency variables and with low socio-economic status, unemployed males and overcrowding, were both sets of variables highly associated with the same factor.

Canonical analysis has been proposed as a means of improving this kind of approach and of identifying more specific relationships among delinquency and census variables. As a technical procedure to avoid intercorrelation within sets of variables, Gittus and Stephens (1973) suggested that factor scores, obtained from factor analyses of the two data sets, should be used as inputs to canonical analysis. This strategy was followed in Cardiff and Table 5.3 summarizes the varimax factors from which scores were derived. For the 1966 delinquency variables, three leading factors are labelled as more serious offences by older males, less serious offences by younger juveniles, and female offenders committing larceny; for 1971 the same three dimensions are identified. For the 1966 census variables, the three leading factors are labelled socio-economic status, housing substandardness, and family status; 1971 factors are again very similar. The canonical analysis uses factor scores as

Table 5.3 Factor loadings for delinquency and census variables, Cardiff 1966 and 1971

	VARIMAX FACTORS					
	1966			**1971**		
	1	**2**	**3**	**1**	**2**	**3**
DELINQUENCY						
1. All offenders	0.55	0.51	*0.59*	0.75	*0.54*	
2. More serious	0.70		*0.49*		*0.89*	
3. Less serious	0.34	0.79	*0.32*	0.89		
4. Males	0.83	0.41		0.73	*0.58*	
5. Females		0.49	*0.65*	0.43		0.79
6. Aged 10–14		0.87		0.85		
7. Aged 15–19	0.78		*0.45*	0.46	*0.73*	0.27
8. Against person					*0.79*	
9. Against property	0.75	0.30		0.35		
10. Larceny	0.35	0.57	*0.60*	0.82	*0.38*	
11. Cautioned		0.77		0.87		
12. Fined	0.44		*0.80*	0.32	*0.86*	
13. Probation	0.46					
14. Care					0.60	0.48
15. Males 15–19	0.90			0.53	0.66	
16. All 10–17	0.57	0.67		0.82	0.34	
% variance	28.8	22.9	15.6	35.3	28.5	07.6
CENSUS						
1. Sex ratio	0.27					*0.31*
2. 10–19 years	*0.26*	0.32	*0.75*	*0.37*		0.76
3. Foreign-born				0.79		
4. Shared dwelling		*0.70*	0.45	0.87		
5. No amenities	*0.39*	0.82		0.57	*0.64*	
6. Owner-occupiers	0.73		0.41		0.36	0.36
7. Local authority tenants	*0.67*	0.55		*0.53*	*0.33*	0.35
8. Private tenants		*0.81*		0.76		*0.44*
9. Movers within						
10. Movers to Local authority	0.82					
11. Social Class 1 & 2	0.81	0.28			0.87	
12. Social Class 4 & 5	*0.67*	*0.32*			*0.65*	0.36
13. Unemployed males	*0.34*	0.32	*0.33*		0.49	
14. Five or more persons	*0.33*		0.82			0.84
15. Over 1.5 ppr	*0.31*					
16. No fixed bath		0.88		0.47	*0.67*	*0.30*
% variance	21.8	21.5	12.8	20.0	16.9	13.8

For Table 5.3 factor loadings are shown for the three leading Varimax factors only. These are numbered from 1 to 3 in each section of the table though these numbers do not in fact correspond with those in the six and seven factor solutions. Negative loadings are shown in italics.

input to examine relationships between delinquency and census variables in 1966 and 1971. For 1966 the dominant relationship confirmed the familiar link between poor social environment and juvenile offenders. Factors measuring low social class and disadvantaged minorities (foreign-born and unemployed) were associated with most offender factors. This broad relationship was repeated in the 1971 analysis of the two sets of factor scores but in both years no other significant relationship appeared. Each result, therefore, produced only one unambiguous or significant canonical variate and did not specify any relationships beyond the general link with poor environments.

Despite the technical advantages of canonical analysis, it consistently poses problems of interpretation and lack of clarity in results. A simpler regression model has advantages on both these counts in addition to its greater flexibility. A stepwise regression model was used in the Cardiff study with both factor scores and individual census measures as independent variables. The advantage of using factor scores as input is that this procedure helps to overcome problems such as multicollinearity (Hauser, 1975) which arise with stepwise

Table 5.4 Stepwise regression results from factor scores, Cardiff 1966 and 1971

STEP	FACTOR	HIGH LOADINGS	1966			
			S.E.	R²	REG. COEFF.	S.E.
1	7	+Movers into Local authority Social Class 1 & 2 Owner-occupier −Social Class 4 & 5 Local Authority tenants	13.7	0.12	−5.10	0.25
2	3	+Foreign born unemployed males	12.8	0.24	−5.10 4.94	1.17 1.17
3	5	−Sex ratio	11.9	0.34	−5.10 4.94 4.65	1.09 1.09 1.09
4	2	−No bath No amenities Private tenants Share dwelling	11.7	0.37	−5.10 4.94 4.65 −2.41	1.07 1.07 1.07 1.07
			1971			
1	3	+Overcrowding unemployed males	1.7	0.15	0.71	0.16
2	5	+Owner-occupiers Social Class 1 & 2				
2	5	+Unemployed males Foreign born −Sex ratio	1.6	0.27	0.71 0.64	0.15 0.15
3	2	+No amenities No bath Share dwelling −Social Class 1 & 2	1.5	0.36	0.71 0.64 0.54	0.14 0.14 0.14

s.e. = standard error
A square root transformation was applied to the 1971 dependent variable

regression. Varimax scores for seven factors in 1966 and six in 1971 from the census variables, formed the independent variables with overall delinquency rate as the dependent variable. Table 5.4 shows the factors (with highest loadings to aid interpretation) associated with each step of the regression procedure, produced in decreasing order of importance. The first step for 1966 identifies the main social class dimension negatively linked with delinquency; the second step shows positive links with the disadvantaged minorities; the third step positive links with an excess of males; and the fourth step similar positive associations with substandard housing. For 1971 results are very similar and the three steps shown in Table 5.4 indicate a negative link with social class, positive with disadvantaged minorities, and positive with substandard housing. Results from these regressions are clear

Table 5.5 Stepwise regression results from independent variables, Cardiff 1966 and 1971

STEP	VARIABLE	1966			
		S.E.	R²	REG. COEFF.	S.E.
1	13:unemployed males	12.1	0.32	2.60	0.35
2	12:Social Class 4 & 5	11.6	0.37	1.81	0.43
				0.32	0.10
3	1:sex ratio	11.5	0.39	1.76	0.42
				0.24	0.11
				−1.67	0.77
4	2:aged 0–19	11.3	0.42	1.70	0.42
				0.27	0.11
				−1.89	0.77
				−0.24	0.13
5	10:movers	11.2	0.43	1.82	0.42
				0.18	0.12
				−1.77	0.77
				−0.30	0.13
				−1.96	1.11
		1971			
1	13:unemployed males	1.6	0.31	0.40	0.06
2	18:lone parents	1.5	0.37	0.29	0.06
				0.13	0.04
3	1:sex ratio	1.5	0.40	0.23	0.07
				0.12	0.04
				−0.40	0.16
4	10:movers	1.4	0.42	0.23	0.07
				0.11	0.04
				−0.38	0.16
				−0.06	0.03
5	4:share dwelling	1.4	0.44	0.21	0.07
				0.11	0.04
				0.35	0.13
				−0.08	0.03
				0.24	0.13

s.e.= standard error
A square root transformation was applied to the 1971 dependent variable.

and show strong associations of delinquency residence with several facets of an essentially poor social and physical urban environment.

As a follow-up to regression using factor scores as independent variables, suitably transformed individual census variables were used as input, again with overall delinquency rate as the dependent variable. In order to take account of the caveats of intercorrelation, pair-wise coefficients were scanned and in fact only two had values of above 0.8. For both 1966 and 1971 male unemployment rate proved to be the most diagnostic independent variable, accounting in each case for just over 30 per cent of the total variance. Low socio-economic status (variable 12) was the second-ranked variable in 1966 and lone parent (variable 18), which was not available for 1966, held this rank in 1971. Scanning the whole list (Table 5.5), delinquency is positively associated with high unemployment, an excess of males, low social class, broken homes and shared dwellings, and is negatively associated with high social class and good housing conditions. Of the approaches used in Cardiff, regression provides the most useful and clear results.

These Cardiff results have been reported in some detail as confirmation of the relationship between delinquency residence and a poor environment. In general terms this relationship has been demonstrated consistently by many studies using a variety of methodologies and is an established fact in the context of known offenders. Results tend to show connections with indicators of both social and built environments but the former are clearly of greater significance. These associations with the poor environment can be conceptualized in a number of ways and of these the framework of a cycle of poverty or deprivation has been most widely used (Rutter and Madge, 1976). Figure 5.4 illustrates this cycle and the way in which various disadvantages of the poor environment – housing condition, social and economic opportunities, climate of opinion – affect the life chances of the individual. Poverty, the central feature of the cycle, arises from low occupational skills and poor education; the resultant inability to compete in the housing market places households in less advantageous tenure conditions; poor access to urban facilities and to favourable moral influences and opportunities compound the difficulties and lead the next generation back into the cycle. The cycle of poverty can clearly be seen in an over-mechanistic way and there are many exceptions, but it does provide a framework within which the various facets of poor environment can be contexted and the likelihood of delinquency as one 'output' conceived.

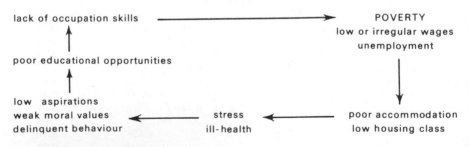

5.4 The cycle of poverty.

Hypothesis type 3: Territorial social indicators and a theory of competitive markets

The third set of hypotheses arising from studies of ecological association is both the most recent and the most tentative. It may, however, have wider implications which would allow research findings from this type of investigation to be linked with studies at other levels of analysis, in particular with that concerned with the structural origins of local social problems. This type of hypothesis can first be exemplified from the Sheffield crime project (Baldwin and Bottoms, 1976). With reference to an earlier concept developed by Rex and Moore (1967), a housing class hypothesis was suggested which argues that crime rates are lower among residents of owner-occupied housing than of rented tenure groups. On examining the proposition that this variation was simply a reflection of social class differences, Baldwin and Bottoms found that for adult male offenders the link between tenure group and offender rates remained even when socio-economic status differences were controlled. They concluded that in considering the pattern of adult male offender rates it was essential to bear in mind the type of tenure area in addition to social class.

This hypothesis was tested using data for Cardiff in 1966 and 1971. Following the same procedure as in Sheffield, enumeration districts were classified as owner-occupied, local authority rented, private rented and mixed. For the first three categories the classification requirements were that over half of the households should fall into the particular tenure group. Table 5.6 (A) shows the mean offender rates for each of three subgroups by four classes of tenure in Cardiff. In each case it is clear that offender rates in the owner-occupier group are well below the city average and are substantially below those recorded for other tenure groups. Highest offender rates occur in the private rented sector (though it should be noted that numbers of enumeration districts in this group are small) and are also relatively high on local authority estates. Table 5.6(B) also shows the results of testing the partial correlation coefficients among five variables, three of which describe tenure groups and two the social class composition of the small areas.

As a test of independence of socio-economic status effects, these results offer some support for the housing class hypothesis. At the 5 per cent level of significance, the correlation between low delinquency rate and owner-occupance remains valid even when social class effects are controlled. This is true of three offender rates though neither of the rented tenure groups hold significant relationships with offender rates when social class is controlled. The limited housing class hypothesis which can be supported from this analysis is that owner-occupiership appears to have some influence on offender rates regardless of social

Table 5.6 Offender rates by housing class in Cardiff

	COUNCIL	RENTED	OWNER-OCCUPIED	MIXED	ALL
(A) MEAN RATES					
Number of EDs	28	14	64	13	119
Male 10 to 19	40	59	24	39	33
Female 10 to 19	11	13	6	12	9
Male 15 to 19	63	90	35	66	51
(B) PARTIAL CORRELATIONS		1.4	2.5	3.5	
(a) All offenders	10–19	−0.20*	0.06	0.11	
(b) Male offenders	10–19	−0.20*	0.00	−0.04	
(c) Female offenders	10–19	−0.12	0.15	−0.02	
(d) Male offenders	15–19	−0.22*	0.08	0.08	

* Significant at the 5 per cent level
Offender rates are shown as number of known juvenile offenders per 1000 population at risk.
1. Owner-occupiers. 2. Council tenants. 3. Private renters. 4. High Social Class. 5. Low Social Class.
ED = Enumeration district

class variations. Although plausible reasons for this influence can be formulated (that is, ownership of property increases interest in the maintenance of law and order or such areas are viewed more benevolently by the law enforcers), they can only be conjectural until the hypothesis has been more comprehensively tested.

Bearing in mind the caveats of inferring meaningful relationships from statistical evidence, it is still possible to develop an argument which sees links between an indicator such as tenure or housing class and national and societal rather than local conditions. Housing classes can be variously regarded in conceptual terms but form one outcome of the conflict for resources and the ability of individual households to obtain access to better 'goods'. As has been argued elsewhere (Herbert, 1975), indicators should be theory-based and one framework is that offered by the concept of key competitive markets. If tenure is really a source of variation in offender rates and a reliable indicator of housing class, then some direct link between local outcomes and their 'structural' origins can be postulated.

There are other indicators which may have similar status. In all the statistical analyses which have been reported for Cardiff, unemployed males has emerged as a key indicator of offender rates. This finding is by no means particular to Cardiff or to the United Kingdom. In Schmid's (1960) widely cited analysis of Seattle, a main variable in his crime dimension was unemployed males. Unemployment occurs in areas of low socio-economic status and in areas occupied by ethnic minorities, and though not independent of these variables it is in itself the most explicit indicator of a failure to compete in the employment market. All the indications in Western society are that youth unemployment is rising and that the problem is particularly acute among British immigrant groups and the black population in America. A link between this indicator and delinquency is therefore an indictment of a social system which produces large-scale unemployment and denies a basic right to work. Figure 5.5 draws some of these ideas together in a framework which includes education as a third competitive market (Herbert, 1975). The thrust of the diagram is to link local conditions via bureaucratic controls and 'gatekeepers' to their structural origins.

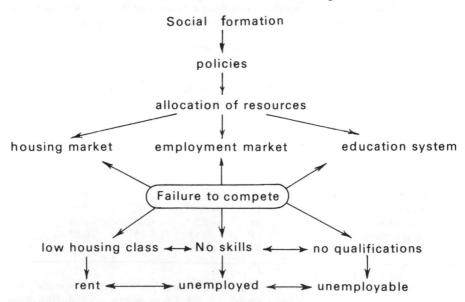

5.5 Social indicators and a theory of competitive markets; the concept could also be phrased in terms of access to scarce resources.

Some qualification can be stated in respect of this line of argument. Firstly, individual responses to these macro conditions are variable and nothing mechanistic should be read into Figure 5.5. Secondly, there are (in common with hypothesis type 1) dangers of drawing too much inference from statistical associations. It is suggested however that indicators which appear persistently over a range of studies and have some theory-base should not be dismissed. At least they identify *issues*, such as poor tenure circumstances and lack of employment, which warrant closer attention in relation to offenders and criminality. If, for example, it can be shown that high rates of youth unemployment can lead to vandalism and petty crime, this has to be recognized as a *cost* of policy decisions which lead to plant closures and redundancy. Similarly, if owner-occupance can be shown to engender attitudes more amenable to 'order' and non-offenders, then policies which enable the spread of this type of tenure should be considered a benefit. These are preliminary thoughts on complex issues but they do offer some evidence that ecological analysis with all its limitations, can be related to other levels of analysis.

INVESTIGATING THE SUBJECTIVE ENVIRONMENT

A further way forward from areal and ecological analyses of offender data is that of studying individual areas in greater depth. Initial results for Cardiff suggested that the poor environment model in itself was partial and insufficient. As suggested earlier, not all those inner-city districts and public housing projects which could be categorized as 'poor environments' did in fact have high delinquency rates. The two possibilities are that there are variations in the details of the 'objective' environment, such as social class composition, which account for the differences, or that 'subjective' variations occur. For the Cardiff study it was hypothesized that the latter situation would occur. Figure 5.6 sets this hypothesis in a framework which suggests a juxtaposition of 'structural' and local environmental concepts. As it was used in the Cardiff study the hypothesis can be stated in two parts.

1. Variations in the subjective environment underpin variations in delinquency rates among local groups and areas.
2. Some kind of neighbourhood effect occurs which conceptually can be linked with subcultural theory.

A research strategy for Cardiff was developed with this hypothesis in mind. An area sampling framework was formed from a principal components analysis of forty census

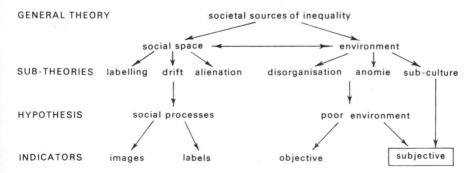

5.6 Contexts for a subjective environment hypothesis.

Table 5.7 Area sampling in Cardiff

(A) Characteristics of the sample areas;

AREA	ED	GENERAL	FERTILITY* RATIO	SHARE* DWELLING	OWNER† OCCUPIER	LA† TENANTS	SOCIAL CLASS† I & II	V
Adamsdown	260 516	Terraced row	61.0	23.3	40.6	0.0	9.2	34.2
Canton	260 314	Terraced row	50.0	22.2	65.4	2.5	8.2	25.9
Ely	260 402	Council estate	42.1	0.0	9.4	88.5	4.9	25.2
Llanrumney	260 120	Council estate	66.2	3.2	1.2	97.6	3.6	38.9
Mynachdy	260 303	Council estate	33.3	0.1	2.4	95.3	5.6	24.3
Rhiwbina	263 113	Private suburb	37.0	0.1	92.2	0.1	45.5	1.5

Notes: All figures are percentages and were derived from the 1966 Sample Census, which was the latest data source available at the preparation stage of the research.

* Ratio was calculated as $\dfrac{\text{children aged } 0-4}{\text{females aged } 15-44} \times \dfrac{100}{1}$

† These indices refer to households. LA = Local authority.

(B) Composition of sample populations by areas

AGE OF CHIEF EARNER	NON-DELINQUENT			DELINQUENT		
	M	C	R	A	E	L
20–24	2	4	0	1	2	7
25–34	19	29	22	9	24	18
35–44	11	21	38	18	22	28
45–54	22	16	16	23	18	29
55–64	26	14	14	21	11	8
65+	13	10	4	18	12	1
not known	7	6	6	10	11	9

(a) 5.4 (6df) not significant

HOUSEHOLD SIZE

	M	C	R	A	E	L
1	3	2	0	4	1	1
2	36	17	16	34	16	4
3	16	36	22	20	21	17
4	16	28	38	19	17	21
5	18	12	16	8	15	29
6	9	3	4	8	13	16
7 or more	2	2	4	7	7	12

(a) 27.0 (7df) significant $p = 0.01$

SOCIAL CLASS

	M	C	R	A	E	L
AB	0	1	34	1	1	1
C_1	9	7	40	14	3	9
C_2	39	53	22	30	19	38
D	35	19	2	37	46	28
E	17	20	2	18	31	24

(b) 9.6 (4df) not significant $p = 0.01$

Notes: Social class typology: AB managerial/administrative or professional; C_1 supervisory or clerical; C_2 skilled manual; D semi or unskilled manual, E lowest levels of subsistence.

Abbreviations used for area names: M (Mynachdy); C (Canton); R (Rhiwbina); A (Adamsdown); E (Ely); L (Llanrumney) e) *A:E:L.* The letters (a) to (e) indicate

Chi-square tests: (a) delinquent areas compared with non-delinquent areas, i.e. MCR:AEL; (b) MC:AEL; (c) M:C:AEL; (d) M:C:R; (e) A:E:L. The letters (a) to (e) indicate the relevant chi-square testing format in each of the tables.

df = degrees of freedom

variables (Herbert and Evans, 1974). Main dimensions to emerge included socio-economic status, tenure and housing, substandardness and familism; scores from these formed the input to a cluster analysis which classified the enumeration districts into 'social areas'. The second element of the area sampling framework came from the offender rates for 1966 and 1971. From this framework, the aim was to select areas for detailed investigation including three areas with relatively high and three areas with relatively low offender rates (see Fig 5.1(A)). The information on social areas was used to ensure that areas which were contrasted in terms of offender rates, were otherwise very similar. Adamsdown and Canton were both inner-city terraced-row districts but only the former had a high delinquency rate. Ely, Llanrumney and Mynachdy were all public sector housing areas but only the last of these had relatively few offenders. Rhiwbina was a high status suburb with no recorded delinquency; a similar area with high delinquency did not exist. For Rhiwbina the random sample comprised fifty households, in each of the other areas ninety households; interviewers were instructed to omit households which had never had children, but no attempt was made to distinguish on the basis of homes of known offenders.

Table 5.7(A) shows some characteristics of the selected small areas as revealed by key census indicators. Table 5.7(B) shows the actual composition of the sample populations. Canton and Mynachdy had higher social class ratios than expected and there was an over-representation of large families but these differences, arising from the time gap between 1966 census data and the 1973 survey, were not of an order which might invalidate the sampling. Table 5.8(A) shows results for questions designed to establish perceived differences between a delinquent and a non-delinquent area, and these confirm the expected contrasts. To a statistically significant extent, respondents in the non-delinquent area (Canton) regarded their district as containing less crimes and fewer offenders. For the remainder of this section, examples will be restricted to these two inner-city areas and to three aspects of the subjective environment: attitudes to education, parental sanctions for misbehaviour and the definition of serious misbehaviour.

Several theories of delinquency have stressed the importance of attitudes towards education and actual attainment in school (Hargreaves, 1967). Assumptions are that the educational attainments of children are good indicators of the quality of home environment and the opportunities made available. Again, part of Cloward and Ohlin's (1960) argument is that as more legitimate opportunities occur so advancement through accepted societal institutions is made more likely. Table 5.8(B) summarizes the actual attainment levels in Canton and Adamsdown of those children who had left school. This evidence is unambiguous and the non-delinquent area shows a far better record. Table 5.8(B) also shows parental involvement in school activities and again Canton parents emerge more favourably. The interpretation from these figures is that Canton children have advantages in parental attitudes to education which contribute towards a more favourable subjective environment.

There are good reasons to assume that relationships between parents and children are of central importance in understanding delinquent behaviour and that control through 'sanctions' is part of that relationship (Andry, 1960). Parents were asked how they would respond to misbehaviour in a fourteen-year-old boy, the question being phrased in this way to standardize responses. As Table 5.8(C) shows, Canton parents favoured *verbal* sanctions whereas Adamsdown parents resorted more frequently to physical punishment. These differences were again taken as indicative of more favourable attitudes in the non-delinquent area.

The question of defining serious misbehaviour was judged to be particularly relevant to subcultural theory and the hypothesis being tested. For Phillipson (1971), the main contribution of ecology has been that of pointing to the importance of local community characteristics as a natural setting for delinquent values and evidence of this type was sought in

Table 5.8 Comparison of a delinquent and a non-delinquent inner-city area, Cardiff

	CANTON	ADAMSDOWN
	(a)	(b)
(A) PERCEPTION OF AREA		
Places where offenders live		
much better	7	3
better	42	20
average	47	64
worse	2	10
much worse	0	2
don't know	2	1
Places where offences occur		
much better	7	8
better	39	17
average	48	61
worse	6	11
much worse	0	2
don't know	0	1
(B) PARENTAL INVOLVEMENT IN EDUCATION		
Attend evening class		
yes	39	24
no	61	76
Contact with school		
very much	16	5
some	43	23
not much	19	54
none	22	18
Children's qualifications		
none	45	73
up to CSE	3	4
trade	12	9
GCE/OND	23	11
A Level/HND	10	1
College or Degree	7	2
(C) SANCTIONS USED		
Physical	17	38
Verbal	64	48
Deprive of privileges	48	12
Institutional	0	2
(D) ACTS WHICH WOULD BE REPORTED		
Drinking under age	54	31
Taking money from a child	56	21
Taking from school	51	26
Not paying on the bus	38	23
Damaging public property	74	67
Taking drugs	97	82
Taking from cars	84	86
Taking from shops	92	91
Assaulting strangers	97	93

All figures are percentages: chi-squared tests were completed on original data and showed significant differences.

Cardiff. Table 5.8(D) shows responses to a set of questions in which parents were asked to nominate those acts they thought constituted serious misbehaviour; again the question was standardized to a fourteen-year-old boy. All the acts listed are in fact illegal though they do range from relatively minor to serious offences. Over the relatively minor part of the range, the first four offences, Adamsdown parents appeared to condone more misbehaviour and had significantly more tolerant attitudes. The two sets of parents converged over the more serious offences but the contrasts over the blurred area of right and wrong was interpreted as a pointer towards a subcultural effect at this neighbourhood scale. A set of values, more tolerant of delinquent behaviour, is commonly held within Adamsdown which is at variance with that prescribed by society as a whole. For the individual youth the local set of values is likely to be more accessible and relevant.

The results provide support for the original hypothesis. There are systematic variations in subjective environment between the two areas which help towards understanding the differences in delinquency rates. Data have been analysed at an aggregate rather than at an individual scale but do show ways in which subjective indicators can enhance the diagnostic value of more traditional approaches.

THE EMERGENCE OF PROBLEM AREAS

The facts of delinquency areas can be established and their internal characteristics can be examined by detailed surveys; remaining questions concern the emergence and persistence of such areas. These questions are also the most difficult, as their resolution requires historical data of considerable quality and of a type which is rarely available for the inner-city problem areas which have attracted most attention. A more recent British phenomenon is the emergence of problem areas in peripheral urban locations which coincide in part or whole with large public sector housing projects, often of interwar construction. Baldwin (1975b) suggests that in Sheffied the continuing problem of criminality remains, for the most part, in those estates built in the 1930s or earlier; These are the 'problem estates' and are regarded as such by local population, local agencies, social workers and police. The recency of these estates and the fact that they were constructed and documented within the public sector, has made more possible the detailed scrutiny of ways in which they have emerged.

Baldwin (1975b) identified three types of explanation for the emergence of problem estates and assessed the merits of each in the light of the Sheffield study:

1. those theories which focus on allegedly high turnover rates in delinquent estates;
2. suggestions that a paucity of social and recreational facilities for youngsters may lead to problems;
3. suggestions that urban managers have some role in creating problem estates by the criteria they use to allocate tenants to housing in various parts of the city.

Recent research has concentrated on the third type of explanation and has developed this in the more general context of labelling processes. Gill (1977) studying a problem housing project in Liverpool suggested that:

> It was local planning and housing department policies that produced Luke Street. The action of the police and the stereotyping of Luke Street as a 'bad' area were crucial but secondary processes (p. 187).

The longest established argument in support of the view that housing departments create problem estates, is that a 'dumping' policy ensures that tenants, preselected because of adverse qualities, are gathered together on specific estates. Gill (1977) listed some housing officials' descriptions of Luke Street families which included phrases such as 'not suitable for new property', 'suitable for dock area only', 'suitable for West End only', and 'not suitable for corporation to rehouse'. Timms (1965) considered that in Luton the older and less well equipped an estate was, the more likely it would be to serve as a repository for problem families. Whereas individual studies have come to conclusions of this kind, it has proved difficult to demonstrate that such policies have been practised on a large scale. Evidence is not always available, policies change over time and the multitude of considerations which may relate to a particular decision is often difficult to disentangle. The evidence from the Sheffield study (Baldwin, 1975b; Bottoms and Xanthos, 1979) has not been supportive of the dumping theory. Slum clearance tenants had considerable choice among estates in the city, grading was restricted to a small number of properties, and managerial prerogative was limited by the number of vacancies at any one time. It is very likely that 'dumping' has been a past policy in many British cities but there is no clear evidence that it has persisted over long periods of time.

R. Wilson (1963) argues that a self-selection process among potential tenants, based on 'images' of estates and rent levels, works in such a way that most tenants on a problem estate were unconcerned about the level of crime and had no intention of moving though they did feel neglected in terms of housing improvement and maintenance by their municipal landlord. The real problem estate had a very small waiting list of prospective tenants and those existing tenants with any social aspirations were waiting to get off the estate. Tenants who stayed and newcomers accepting vacancies were indifferent to its reputation. Bottoms and Xanthos (1979) in a later study of Sheffield tended to reject the self-selection thesis on the grounds that there was no general evidence of people wishing to move into Botany Bay (the problem estate) unless they had relatives there or were desperate for housing. Gill (1977) recognizes some residential selection process in Luke Street but views it in terms of those least able to compete for housing ending up in the least wanted area.

The question remains of how these estates acquire reputations in the first place. Here the characteristics of the first tenants seem crucial. The Sheffield study showed how one such problem estate was initially used to relocate several notorious gang-leaders and their associates in the 1930s; another suffered from the chance allocation of a couple of families regarded by neighbours as problematic. The important point here is that a downward spiral can begin without any deliberate dumping or grading in th first instance. A further clue from Sheffield was provided from ways in which two estates – one 'problem', the other not – were populated. The better estate had taken its tenants off a long waiting list and largely from a nearby area, the problem estate had been tenanted at a time of low demand by recent applicants to the waiting list from a variety of localities who tended to treat the estate as a short-term option. Facts such as these are not forgotten by the local community and are used to stigmatize the estate.

This idea of stigmatization is important and is linked to the theory that reputations, once established, are perpetuated – perhaps undeservedly – because the area is *labelled* as problematic. Damer's (1974) study of a Glasgow housing development is the most detailed case study of this kind so far published. His 'Wine Alley', built in 1934 with just over 500 dwellings and a population of 2000, has an atrocious reputation with local people and officialdom alike. Damer, using the anthropological approach of observation and involvement (he lived in the area for a significant length of time), found it to be a fairly ordinary Glasgow manual workers' community. Its emergence as a problem estate was strongly tied to its recruitment of occupants from distant parts of the city, and resentment of this fact by local Govan population. Municipal officials stereotyped Wine Alley as a place typified by rent arrears, vandalism, crime and socio-psychological problems. Its persistence was aided

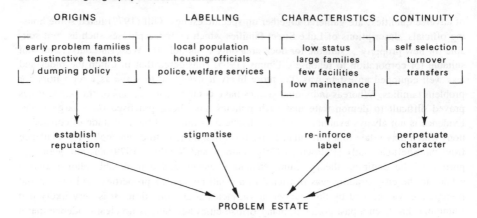

5.7   Contributory factors in the emergence and persistence of problem estates.

by its physical identity and clear boundaries but was primarily a product of labelling on the grounds of past perceptions rather than modern realities of its occupants' behaviour. Gill (1977) found much in Luke Street to support this evidence.

Analyses of the emergence of problem estates have highlighted a number of interrelated social processes which contribute to their existence. Figure 5.7 summarizes these. Although a large number of factors are involved, the key elements appear to be public housing policy, self-selection among tenants and labelling. The elements in Figure 5.7 and some of its central hypotheses can now be examined with reference to one problem estate in Cardiff for which a limited amount of information is available.

The Ely estate, which in 1971 comprised 4200 dwelling units and housed over 14 000 people, qualifies for the description of a problem area on a number of counts. It was, on the basis of mapping offender residences from several data sources (see Herbert, 1976), a delinquency area. It possesses a poor reputation within Cardiff as will be shown, and the emergence of this reputation can be traced over time. Land for the new estate was acquired in 1920 and 3412 dwellings had been completed by 1929. A chronic problem was the lack of facilities and the estate remains poorly served in this respect. Largely as a result of changing standards over time, the houses compare unfavourably with those on newer estates; many of the first-phase dwelling units in Ely, for example, have no inside toilet. First occupants of Ely were drawn from the crowded area of the inner city, principally from the districts of Grangetown, Splott and Canton. These people were often Catholics and from the most substandard parts of the old city.

> They were not ''Chapel'' or ''Church'' and attended Catholic schools. They had strange names that all began with O' or Mac, they belonged to large families, they tended to be poorly dressed and were dangerous if provoked. Their homes were often the rent collector's nightmare, and occasionally poverty would drive them to bizarre behaviour' (Denning, 1973).

There was a record of minor gang warfare in these early days, and a well-documented incident of vandalism involving newly planted trees. Ely, then, grew with problems, some were the production of inadequacies of design and provision, others were imported with sections of its early population. It has a reputation as a problem estate which matches its modern high relative rates of delinquency:

Ely, one of the largest housing estates in Cardiff, does not have a lot going for it. It has poor social facilities for young and old, not enough open space, traffic problems and poor shopping. Among the key problems facing the district are truancy, vandalism and delinquency (*South Wales Echo*, 1975).

This historical material provides partial support for the hypothesis concerning delinquent traditions in particular estates; more direct evidence was obtained from a direct survey of residential areas in Cardiff (Herbert, 1976). Respondents drawn from six contrasted areas in the city were asked to name any three Cardiff districts to which they would definitely not wish to move. As Figure 5.8 shows, Ely was by far the least favoured of the council estates, with 46 per cent of respondents including it in their nominations. Among

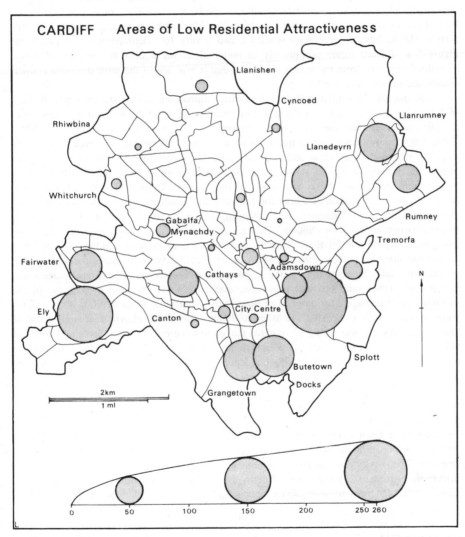

5.8 Areas of low residential attractiveness in Cardiff. Number of people nominating a low preference for each area are shown. Source: Herbert (1979) p. 133.

respondents from the four low-income areas in the sample, excluding Ely, nomination rates for Ely ranged from 51 to 74 per cent. When asked to give reasons for their nomination of the single least desired area, comments made in respect of Ely related to its remoteness, the fact that it was 'very rough' and 'dirty' and, for one at least, it was a 'little Chicago'. Ely is now clearly stigmatized as a problem estate in Cardiff, though it is of course in no way comparable to the bad areas of places like Glasgow and Belfast. Social processes mentioned earlier, such as housing policy and tenant selection, are likely contributory mechanisms and although there is a reasonable level of satisfaction among Ely residents, to outside eyes the image is bad and observable behaviour is confirmatory.

The next question which arises in relation to the hypothesis for this section concerns the 'climate of opinion' within Ely and the significance this might have in understanding its high modern levels of delinquent behaviour. To probe this question, further data from the Cardiff survey are used and another council estate, Mynachdy, is used as a basis for comparison. Mynachdy, from official statistics, had a very low delinquency rate and, from Figure 5.8, did not figure prominently in nominations for undesirable residential areas. Anecdotal evidence from the survey suggested that it was one of the most desirable council estates and possessed a good image.

Material used is similar to that in the earlier comparison of the two inner-city districts of Adamsdown and Canton and Table 5.9 summarizes information obtained from questions designed to investigate the subjective environments of the two estates (Herbert, 1975). Table 5.9(A) shows responses to questions on ways in which people perceived their estates as places where offences occur and as places where offenders live, in both cases relative to other Cardiff districts. Results show strong contrasts between the two estates with, in Ely, a considerable awareness of the bad image of the district. Table 5.9(B) explores parental attitudes towards education as a criterion for assessing good, positive home influence. It is clear that if interest in education and schooling is a measure, Ely parents provide a poor social environment for their children. They are little involved in school activities, have low educational aspirations for their children, and 80 per cent of their children who had left school had done so without formal qualifications. Table 5.9(C) compares parental control on the two estates by comparing stated responses to misbehaviour. Ely parents make much less use of verbal sanctions and more use, markedly so in the case of truancy, of the institution as a surrogate for parental responsibility. Finally in Table 5.9(D), when parents were presented with a checklist and asked to define serious misbehaviour, it is clear that at the margins of right and wrong Ely parents tended to have more lax standards and codes of behaviour. At all points in this table which tests a number of attitudes indicated by the research literature as related to the incidence of delinquent behaviour, Ely compares unfavourably with Mynachdy.

Although the historical evidence is fragmentary, there are numerous clues to the understanding of Ely's early acquisition of a poor reputation and its persistence over time. The first tenants were of a different 'kind' to the general population of the city and early incidents have been magnified in significance. Certainly some kind of general labelling persists, as Fig. 5.8 illustrates, and this probably mirrors the attitudes of many official agencies. The survey data are generally indicative of a set of values within the estate which underpins its measurably high rates of delinquency. As with the Adamsdown example discussed earlier, there is some evidence for a subcultural effect within this problem estate.

SUMMARY

This chapter has reviewed the status of some of the concepts and generalizations relevant to

Table 5.9 Comparison of a delinquent and a non-delinquent estate, Cardiff

	MYNACHDY	ELY
	(a)	(b)
(A) PERCEPTION OF AREAS		
Places where offenders live		
much better	14	0
better	38	6
average	45	53
worse	1	33
much worse	0	1
don't know	2	7
Places where offences occur		
much better	16	0
better	40	4
average	41	56
worse	1	31
much worse	0	3
don't know	2	6
(B) PARENTAL INVOLVEMENT IN EDUCATION		
Attend evening class		
yes	35	20
no	65	80
Contact with school		
very much	22	1
some	35	32
not much	25	32
none	18	35
Childrens' qualifications		
none	59	83
up to CSE	1	0
trade	24	8
GCE/OND	12	7
A level/HND	1	1
College or degree	3	1
(C) SANCTIONS USED		
Physical punishment	19	21
Verbal	51	23
Deprive of privileges	28	43
Institutional	6	15
Ignore	8	21
(D) ACTS WHICH WOULD BE REPORTED		
Drinking under age	36	47
Taking money from a child	50	40
Taking from school	57	31
Not paying on the bus	38	17
Damaging public property	80	73
Taking drugs	91	94
Taking from cars	82	85
Taking from shops	88	92
Assaulting strangers	89	97

All figures are percentages; chi-squared tests were completed on original data and showed significant differences.

the analysis of offenders in urban areas and has provided examples from a particular British city. The spatial generalizations based on American experience are clearly in need of significant modification, as the bases on which simple centre/periphery contrasts were predicated have changed. Spatial analysis can be applied at a variety of urban scales from offender rates for small areas to distributions of homes of individual offenders. This kind of analysis has real value in establishing frameworks of area studies, in portraying the existence of 'problem' areas, and in suggesting some hypotheses on spatial interaction, but space in itself has little independent significance and needs to be contexted in its social meanings. Much of the research into ecological associations of offender rates is redundant and is certainly characterized by high levels of repetition, despite the increasingly sophisticated methodologies. The summary of this type of research, however, has classified its findings in terms of three types of hypotheses. Whereas the first of these, with its links with traditional theories of crime, is often guilty of drawing too many inferences from statistical correlations, the second is mainly descriptive and as such has value in depicting the nature of urban problems, and the third offers some promise of a format which links indicators of local social conditions to the structural situations from which they have originated. It is admitted that the last type of hypothesis courts the hazards of the first and should be used in qualified ways.

Much of the past research record concerned with offenders in urban environments has rested upon official statistics and objective indicators. A case has been argued for a focus upon the subjective environment and for data, both quantitative and qualitative, of a rather different kind. This type of research should proceed from theories such as subculture and should not depend so heavily on official definitions of offenders. The meaning of official statistics should be examined and social issues such as fear of victimization, attitudes towards police and policing, and the interaction of police, offender, and victim investigated. Questions raised on the origins of problem areas push research back into a level of analysis 'above' local environment involving urban managers, decision-makers, and the allocative processes. This direction is one which analyses of other issues should also follow.

CHAPTER 6
RESEARCH DIRECTIONS AND POLICY IMPLICATIONS: SOME CONCLUSIONS

INTRODUCTION

This concluding chapter has several objectives. Firstly, it offers a brief summary of those findings of criminological research and of recent more explicitly spatial studies which together contribute towards some basis from which a geography of crime in cities can be developed. Secondly, some of the policy implications of this kind of research will be assessed, and thirdly, some of the future directions for study will be discussed.

THE FINDINGS OF SPATIAL STUDIES: A SUMMARY

Data and definitions

In preceding chapters, the need to maintain a distinction between the study of offence and offender rates has been emphasized. Conceptually, it is argued, this is essential because if the focus is on the local conditions within which criminality occurs, offences and offenders need to be related to different environmental qualities. For offences, the local environment must be seen in terms of the opportunities it presents, the deterrents it appears to offer, and the ways in which the offender intrudes on the behavioural space of others. For offenders, local environment has less dominant significance in the larger order of life chances and the individual's place in society, but it does contain the important reference groups of home residential area, and locality-based activities which must have significance in understanding who offends and who does not. Both offences and offenders are amenable to geographical perspectives but it may well be that the former, less enmeshed in a palimpsest of contradictory causation theories, provides the more fruitful avenue for research attention by geographers. Although geographers undoubtedly need to widen their perspectives and examine macro as well as micro forces in society, the situational contexts within which offence patterns can be analysed demand methodologies closer to those with which they are most familiar.

There may also be practical advantages in this kind of emphasis in an emerging geography of crime. Where an offence is committed is a less confidential and sensitive item of information than is that of who the offenders are. In a research area where access to data is a problem this point is not insignificant. Again, in a situation in which official statistics have to form an important input to many analyses, the data bases on offences are generally more comprehensive than those on offenders. This will vary from one kind of offence to another depending on the type of crime, the priority which police allocate to it in terms of manpower and the resultant detection rate. An awareness of the problems of data and definition concerning both offences and offenders must pervade all kinds of research and the knowledge that only about one-sixth of all crime is likely to come to the notice of authority and that clear-up rates average around 40 per cent puts the data issues into perspective.

Despite their shortcomings, official statistics have roles to play and from a geographer's point of view the territorial units for which these figures are published is of prime importance. At present the areal units for crime statistics are generally too gross to be of any practical value. British *Criminal Statistics* are especially limited in this respect and the problem has increased with the mergers of police forces to produce even larger units in the 1970s. The problem of matching police districts to any other data source is considerable and renders most types of statistical analysis a mammoth exercise. In the United States the *Uniform Crime Reports* have better data bases, but these remain relatively gross in terms of area observations. Some issues on official data will be raised below but the general point to be made at this stage is that some form of disaggregated spatial data would be invaluable for research purposes. It is only within the last two decades that census data have become easily available as small area statistics; this has had an enormous effect on research generated in both governmental institutions and academic communities. Clearly similar small area statistics could, without breach of confidentiality, provide a valuable data source for crime and delinquency and indeed for other social problems.

Distributions

Areal analysis, in which the distributions over space of offences and offenders are depicted and studied, has figured prominently in the preceding chapters and will remain a basic geographical tool. The value of this type of analysis and the generalizations which it provides can be argued in a number of ways. Firstly, it is important to know where specific problems occur. However much academics may argue about what is a problem and who defines it, there can be little doubt that for the vast majority of people crime is a problem they recognize, dislike, and may live in fear of. If, as has been shown, some groups and some areas in cities carry disproportionate shares of this particular form of social malaise, it is important that the public conscience be stirred and shown what the burden is and on whom it falls. A second, related point is that crime rates, and especially offender rates, have a role in a set of social indicators which provide insights into more general levels of living or social well-being. In this context they form key indices of ways in which the problematics of society surface, along with other indices such as mental illness, ill-health and educational disadvantage (D. M. Smith, 1974; Knox, 1975).

Thirdly, it can be argued that their roles as 'indicators' help understand the stability or otherwise of spatial generalizations and 'models' of crime rates. The inner city/outer city contrast evident in American cities for crime rates of most kinds, for example, reflects the general distribution of poverty and wealth, high and low density, bad and good quality housing, black and white populations. American suburban municipalities have consistently and successfully resisted pressures for change and the distribution of crime continues to mirror a largely stable social geography. British cities on the other hand have undergone structural changes resulting from the injection of strong welfare criteria into a competitive housing market and the large-scale construction of public sector estates. Given this situation of change, simple areal patterns of zones and gradients no longer exist as crime rates respond to a new social geography of the city.

This point can be elaborated with reference to some of the Cardiff evidence. A number of territorial social indicators, derived from a theory of competitive markets or access to scarce resources, was mapped from 1971 census data (Herbert, 1975). Substandard housing was largely confined to the central city but disadvantage in employment and education showed up strongly in peripheral as well as in central locations. Substandard housing occurs in residual inner city areas and in early public housing projects where modern standards were not met. There is success, for public policy, therefore, in raising the quality of the built environment, but this is not paralleled in the social environment. Modern council estates remain similar to inner-city terraces in terms of socio-economic status and educational attainment; they also continue to show high offender rates, suggesting a transference of behaviour and a disadvantaged social environment of little change. The message here is that social disadvantage is redistributed spatially and delinquency continues to be an expression of that disadvantage, albeit in different territorial form.

Areal analyses of offender rates show that these respond to a changing residential structure which in turn mirrors the broader societal forces which allocate power and resources. It is in this context that one of the central messages of the radical critique must be accepted. The geography of crime is in many ways a predictable outcome of a society which produces inequalities and rewards differentially. Local outcomes, be they problem areas or disadvantaged groups, need to be related to the macro-forces which underlie them. This provides a necessary but not a sufficient statement in seeking to understand the incidence of crime and the distribution of offenders. It is necessary because it does identify a critical context; it is not sufficient because it does not explain the considerable variability in response to these macro conditions. This variability may in part by induced by the way in which the system defines the problem and provides the data, but there is ample evidence from self-report and victimization studies, not based on official statistics, to testify to its reality in more general terms. In the same way as traditional criminological theory has identified poverty and disadvantage as conditions which *may* lead to criminal behaviour, so the forces which in turn produce poverty and disadvantages have influential but not mechanistic roles. Between the 'system' and its outcomes are many mediating factors, the effects of these need to be considered and give the question of understanding crime both its complexity and its elusiveness. Areal analyses of crime and offenders must work in these terms. There is no geometry of space which has a meaning independent of the socio-political forces, or indeed of the morphological and land-use contexts, of which it is part.

In any inventory of useful spatial generalizations on crime patterns Shaw and McKay's (1942) summary of concentric zones and gradients must retain a central place. Based on official statistics and known offenders, this model stood the test of time for a number of decades and still keeps some value as a broad generalization and pedagogic device. American cities with their 'simple' social geographies retain the model most clearly, elsewhere different social geographies are reflected in distortions to the model. Public sector housing causes distortions in many European cities; Third World cities reveal a much greater complexity which reflects a greater admixture of land-uses and localized clusters of population groups. De Fleur's (1967) identification of dispersed clusters of offenders in shanties and servant quarters has parallels in early stages of American urban development (Radford, 1979). At an aggregate scale of analysis this type of spatial generalization can be made and some research into the form of these generalizations outside the well-studied American and Western European contexts remains a necessity.

Other spatial generalizations on crime are not well developed. The concept of the delinquency area can be recognized as one attempt to fill the gap between the urban and individual scales of analysis. The proposition, simply stated, is that within larger cities there exist identifiable districts which house disproportionate shares of known offenders. Historically such delinquency areas – and earlier crime areas – have been restricted to inner-city areas of high density, substandardness, and poverty; in modern times the 'problem estates' provide equivalents. This 'equivalence' has to be treated with caution. Delinquency areas emerge as those districts with relatively more offenders *within* a given city. In absolute terms the delinquency areas of modern Cardiff bear no comparison with the crime area of early nineteenth-century Merthyr (Strange, 1980), nor with the modern delinquency areas of Belfast or Glasgow. Data availability is a considerable constraint but detailed inter-urban comparisons involving a large number of cities are essential to set the concept of delinquency areas in proper perspective.

Within neighbourhoods, at the scale of individual offenders, very few areal analyses have been attempted. The few available studies (Morris, 1957) point to street by street variations and highly localized clusters within larger districts. Evidence from Cardiff suggests that such clusters and the notion of 'black' and 'white' streets is real enough. Even over a limited period of one year, individual households produced two or more offenders and seem to have some catalyst effect. However, idea of a spatial clustering of individual offenders within the neighbourhood which corresponds with a delinquent group could not be sustained. Residential neighbourhood appeared to provide a general milieu within which selective relationships established at other points of conflux such as school, club or interest group, usually among close age-cohorts, were continued. American research into teenage gangs in cities (Ley, 1974), although rarely plotting homes of individual gang members, does suggest close alignment of gangs with geographical space and territories within the inner city. Research on the spatial behaviour of individual offenders can most usefully be developed with a focus on interaction and upon the networks which are built around a variety of points of conflux. Work by some American geographers on movements of offenders is preliminary but may develop into analysis of greater depth and insight.

This summary has so far focused on patterns of offenders and in so doing has reflected the bias in the literature. Areal analyses of offences have often tended to replicate those of offenders at an aggregate scale, partly because many offences tended to be committed within home areas and partly because this scale obscures detailed differences. It has been argued that offence patterns are conceptually different because they relate to the opportunity structure which urban environments present. The first general point which can be made is similar to that which applies to offender rates; offence patterns will mirror more general urban geography, and in this context the arrangement of land-use is especially relevant. In Western cities many offences occur in the central area and reflect the opportunities for offences against commercial and business property which the business district offers. 'Downtown' also acts as the focus for many offences against persons such as the assaults and robberies often associated with the meeting places which this area provides.

The other possible generalization has already indirectly been made. This is that a high proportion of crime involves people and property at only small remove from the offender. Many acts of violence are domestic, involving family members or occupants of the same building – people known to each other. In American experience blacks offend against blacks, poor against poor, so crime areas tend to have this more general meaning. Other areal patterns will vary with specific types of offence. Residential burglaries are typical of particular kinds of residential areas, car theft occurs most frequently on larger parking lots, speeding on particular freeways, and so on. At a micro-scale there are vulnerable 'areas', such as the lifts and stairways in some of Newman's high-rise buildings which have yet to be adequately theorized and generalized upon.

Spatial ecology

As spatial ecology has developed replicative studies of patterns of correlation and variable association, it has tended to move into rather sterile ground. Although the methodologies have become more sophisticated, the findings have tended to confirm the correlation of known offenders with poor environments and have not added to our understanding of this relationship in any significant way. Where results have been linked to criminological theories such as social disorganization and anomie, too much inference has often been attempted and the problem of ecological fallacy ignored. It has been argued that the use of statistical associations in theory-testing and development is valid providing the necessary qualifications are made. It has also been suggested that recurrent indices such as male unemployment and housing tenure may be key social indicators which can be related to a more general theory of ability to compete in main 'markets' and to obtain access to scarce resources. A further suggestion is that a move from objective to subjective indicators may add a necessary dimension to the understanding of offender patterns. Areal analysis has been used as a 'means to an end' in the Cardiff example in developing an area sampling framework from which detailed investigations of subjective environments could proceed.

For offences, spatial ecology measuring associations at its traditional aggregate scale is likely to have fewer analytical roles. The need to develop good indices and sensitive risk unit denominators is one such role (Harries, 1980) which will provide a more accurate portrayal of the geography of offences. But it is at the more detailed scales of street, block and individual dwellings that more interesting associations are likely to emerge. Here more social concepts such as opportunity, risk, rewards and familiarity need to be contexted with more objective forms of situational variables. This type of codification can lead to the classification of various types of vulnerable environment but again a focus on the subjective qualities of such environments is likely to add the more telling dimension. Social geographer's research into the meanings attached to place and space provides one avenue for investigation; Carter's (1974) initiative in examining ways in which burglars perceive various 'target' areas deserves development. The idea of interviewing known offenders is well established in criminological research (West, 1967) but their spatial behaviour and urban imagery have never been objects of study.

Geographers have to date played very limited roles in analyses of crime, and spatial qualities have typically emerged as byproducts of criminological research. Some might argue that this accurately reflects the relevance of space but such judgements are premature in the sense that so little analysis has been done that its potential cannot be appreciated. A geographical perspective anyway incorporates far more than is appreciated and the scope is considerable. This summary has focused on spatial qualities evident from available research experience but has also tended to trespass upon what ought to be done. This latter theme will be discussed in more detail at the end of this chapter.

POLICY IMPLICATIONS

Crime rates and comparative study

The link between criminological research and policies designed to reduce the level of crime within society has often been explicit. As crime rates have continued to rise and penal reforms show limited success in reducing crime and recidivism, the justification for research in this context is not always easy to argue. To the extent that crime rates are related to macro trends and forces within society, such as urbanization, industrialisation, the ebbs and flows of economic fortunes and the whole question of equitable distributions of resources, any specific policies related to crime control are likely to have limited impact. Clinard (1978), in a rare attempt at comparative analysis of several Western societies and their criminality, suggested that pronounced differences in crime rates between the United States and Switzerland did not seem to support the general contention that ordinary crime is produced by economic disadvantage or poverty. Clinard's (1978) message seems to be that 'small is beautiful' and his sentiments contain echoes of the garden suburb and new town enthusiasts of the early twentieth century:

> areas of a city with a slum way of life did not develop in Switzerland, and so subsequent generations ... were spared being infected with criminal and other deviant behaviour patterns (p. 156).

Clinard argues that larger cities should aim at an optimal size of 250 000 to 500 000 and that in cities small units of government with approximately 5000 people should assume local citizen responsibility and integrate with youth. Presumably the radical solution has little appeal to Clinard from his observation of the sharply contrasted crime rates of two affluent societies, though several of his recommendations implicitly refer to the different ways in which that affluence is distributed. Comparative research of this kind should be developed in more detail and, as Pahl (1979) argues, there has been far too little comparative analysis of contrasted socialist and capitalist societies. Fundamental transformations of society may have no guarantee of success if fundamentally different societies have crime problems of a similar order. It is interesting that Clinard's study which was conceived as a macro-scale comparison, places considerable emphasis upon micro-scale or locality based solutions to the high crime rates of the United States.

Organization of data

Issues surrounding the definition of offences and the production of official statistics add a further dimension to crime rates and comparisons among different societies. These were discussed at some length in Chapter 1 and need not be considered in detail here. A central academic argument is that criminal statistics are neither neutral nor absolute facts, they have been defined by the data compilers, and those definitions involve subjective judgements which have no explicit theoretical bases. The dangers arise from using criminal statistics in unexamined ways; the ways in which they are defined and their partialness should be exposed. Arising from this is the need to extend research beyond official statistics; white-collar crime, for example, is readily acknowledged but is nowhere near as researched as the 'ordinary' crime to which Clinard (1978) refers. The law itself is a central institution and, although in detail it is continuously under review, its guiding principles of protecting particular sets of interests may have less relevance in the late twentieth century than at the time they were formed. Again, the socio-legal system, including the judiciary and the police, is invested with a great deal of discretionary power. How this power is used and in particular its consistency is of central importance. The policy implications of these issues are far-reaching. They call for a closer and more representative scrutiny of the law-making process and for assurance that where discretionary powers exist they should be applied in uniform monitored ways.

There are more pragmatic policy questions surrounding the form and availability of existing criminal statistics. Despite their problems, official statistics will continue to be central features for much research and there is ample scope, as argued earlier, for greater disaggregation on area bases without infringing any legitimate constraints of confidentiality. A much fuller provision of special tabulations on social, demographic and economic data for police areas would also be a positive advance. At a time when many police forces are turning to computerized access files for different types of offences and categories of offenders, close attention should be paid to locational codes – census small areas and grids – which are added to this system. Data analysis clearly features strongly in many aspects of police work, there are many areas in which research interests in data maintenance, content and access and normal police needs in the prevention and detection of crime can be matched. Pyle ed. (1974) presents several major recommendations relating to criminal statistics and the setting up of a 'criminal justice information system'. Suggestions included the establishment of three basic files relating to location of the offence, details of the victim, and characteristics of the suspect, which should form the main data input with easy computer access. Maximum use of data could be enhanced by the use of computer graphics procedures such as Grids or Symap.

Computer mapping systems have the basic property of displaying specified distributions rapidly. Once data are organized in this manner, however, there are many other possible types of analysis. A range of algorithm models is now available (Rushton, 1979) which enables the solution of optimal location problems, for example, according to specified conditions and constraints. Such a program, developed by geographers at the University of Oklahoma, had been successfully used by the Oklahoma City police department to identify locations for new district police stations. Other districting procedures exist which can be used to define optimal numbers of police patrol areas and specify boundaries. The critical parameters to models of this kind will be subjective – maximum and minimum population size, area, land-use mix – but the methodology which forms an objective stage to these types of policy decisions is nonetheless available. A number of specific recommendations on redistricting were contained in the Harries and Brunn (1978) study of the United States justice system in general and the federal court system in particular. Using a set of court statistics to illustrate variations within states and among regions, they discuss necessary reforms. The broad conclusion was that recent congressional hearings and proposed legislation to realign circuit courts and allocate new judgeships in both circuits, would go a long way towards solving present problems.

Area policies

Policy recommendations arising out of studies of crime in cities have usually been couched in terms of local ameliorative solutions and area policies. The limitations of area policies are well known (Eyles, 1979) and they are never intended to replace policies directed at individuals or households, but as problem areas have consistently been identified, so area policies have their place. The form of such policies revolves round the concept of positive discrimination which allocates more resources to areas of need and recognizes that in particular districts the special services of social workers and educational programmes may be specially needed. Advocacy of area policies and attention to the local conditions in which crime occurs does not abdicate responsibility for the need to recognize and deal with more deeply-rooted causes of inequality and disadvantage, but it does argue that short-term palliatives have their place. Most geographers have advocated working with existing authorities as a practical means of achieving change (Berry, 1972) but this does not mean that more radical attitudes and disengagement are not sometimes essential.

It is interesting to note that Clifford Shaw, in his remedial work in Chicago recognized the issues of this debate (Snodgrass, 1976) and changed his views over time. Shaw worked for many years with the leaders of Chicago Area projects, designed to help inner-city delinquents. His disillusionment with that society and its organizers grew and he increasingly regarded the leaders as those with real responsibility for the city's social problems and his own role as diversionary:

> In an ironic way, the projects protected the property and equipment of the very concerns which were the root causes of disorganization and delinquency' (quoted in Snodgrass, 1976, p. 17).

Shaw's experience provides a rare insight into the dangers of working with the system in too uncritical a way; it is at the point at which obstructionism and lack of scruple become evident that conflict is inevitable. Whereas most 'systems' and their leaders need not be of the kind that Shaw encountered in Chicago, 'liberal' geographers working within the system have the responsibility of recognizing it for what it is worth.

Area policies at the neighbourhood scale are normally achieved through external intervention. This may take the form either of large-scale allocation of funds or resources, or the setting up of an organization of social workers or action teams who attempt to add something to the area. Academic research has consistently underlined the value of such enterprises. The thrust of research findings in Cardiff, for example, is that problem areas tend to suffer from disadvantageous subjective environments in which the prevalent values, moral code, and behaviour form unfavourable 'models' to which youngsters can relate. This idea of a 'neighbourhood effect' suggests that youths growing up in these subjective environments have to cope with easy access to values and examples which could lead them into delinquent behaviour. Other reference groups, such as family and school, may compensate in other directions, but neighbourhood provides a 'contagion' or contaminating effect to be overcome. As a matter for policy, therefore, the general attitudes and activities of residents in problem areas require attention.

Area policies with their substantial external inputs are one means of providing such attention but the other avenue is one which relies more upon the development of internal factors. As many writers have pointed out in the past (Suttles, 1968), social order can exist in objectively deprived circumstances and such neighbourhoods are capable of the type of self-help, involvement and cohesion which Jacobs (1961) has lauded. C. J. Smith (1980) argues that a rebirth of localism and the decentralization of problem-solving are being widely reported in American cities (Suttles, 1975). This trend is stimulating new interest in neighbourhood as a concept and the view of neighbourhood as a humanistic entity is of particular interest. C. J. Smith (1980) classifies a sense of belonging with the image of neighbourhood as home or haven under this heading: a *place* to which individuals relate and are involved with. Sennet's (1973) concept of neighbourhood was stated in very similar terms; for him neighbourhood served as a refuge in a harsh urban world. It is in these kinds of roles that Smith saw some value of neighbourhoods as 'policy-instruments' in the care of the mentally ill:

> Neighbourhoods cannot possibly provide a radical solution for all mental health problems. It is useful to think of neighbourhoods as conservative agents – they provide a haven that can sometimes help to buffer individuals against the stresses they encounter in their personal and civic lives (C. J. Smith, 1980, p. 409).

There is an analogy here for delinquency and crime. Policies which may bring about reversals of presently observed neighbourhood effects in problem areas through a combination of promoted self-help and careful external inputs, provide a climate of opinion in which children are less likely to be diverted into delinquent 'careers'. External and internal forces towards community improvement should be closely interdependent and, as Smith argues, it is possible that help-seeking from within a neighbourhood is indicative of a healthy and positive attitude.

This discussion of the policy implications of research into offenders can be summarized under three headings.

1. At the macro-scale the need is to tackle the roots of inequality in society whether this is a political ethic or a cumbersome and prejudiced bureaucracy. There are questions of whom the law serves (or more importantly whom it does not serve), of definition of criminal behaviour and of the use of discretionary powers in apprehending and sentencing offenders.

2. There is a continued role for area policies designed to upgrade environments, improve

access to resources and facilities and provide a better quality of local living conditions. Such policies require external inputs into particular areas but can work best if they also engender self-help from within.

3 There is the imperative to help individuals in need which is the essential adjunct of any argument for an area policy. Welfare services are organized towards this end and their roles of counselling, monitoring and providing an umbrella of care are critical.

Crime prevention

Research into offences and crime occurrence, closely allied to ideas on crime prevention, has often had explicit policy implications. A number of ideas can be distilled from this research. Firstly, there is a basic classification and codification exercise; local environments which are particularly vulnerable to certain types of offence can be identified at a variety of scales. Secondly, some of the deficiencies, in both physical and social terms, of these environments can be recognized and perhaps rectified. Thirdly, vulnerability in some instances may arise from policing practice and there are more optimal forms and patterns of patrol and service to be implemented. Fourthly, some features of design can be improved and here ideas of defensible space remain of value. In a study of London flats (S. Wilson, 1978), for example, no direct evidence of design influences could be found, but the recommendation was still that future design should include defensible space qualities. From a variety of perspectives, vulnerable areas and situations can be classified and the key variables such as surveillability and cohesiveness can be identified. Physical design factors are relevant but cannot be examined in independence of the social conditions which give them meaning.

Whereas many design improvements can be directed at individual dwellings, spaces and projects, the notion of an area policy based on local community is applicable to offence-prone environments. Measures designed to enhance a sense of belonging, to generate more local involvement, and to create some kind of corporate identity can be protective for potential victims. Such ideas are often denigrated on the grounds that 'neighbourhoods' of this kind do not often exist, but it is precisely in areas faced with some common danger that they have most chance of success. The complacency and non-involvement of middle-class neighbourhoods arises because nothing disturbs that complacency; as Bell and Newby (1978) have argued, when some issue arises 'community' can become 'communion' and bring about the kind of communal identity and action which theorists envisage.

In the United Kingdom, the Home Office allocated funds to a district in Widnes, which had suffered vandalism and petty crime, under its urban aid programme. Residents in the district stood a one in four chance of being burgled in the average year and vandalism was rife. The project involved the clearance of eyesores and development of more play space; overall some thirty-four individual projects were sponsored. Results are very encouraging. Neighbourhood associations have developed to add the dimension of self-help, the burglary rate has been halved, vandalism is down by one-third and damage to telephone kiosks is 12 per cent of its former level. It is difficult to identify which elements of the mix of policies in Widnes were most effective but there seem to be virtues in working on an area basis and supply a 'package' of measures.[1] Key ingredients of this package may include a strengthening of the role of the community in planning and managing its own environment, creating a sense of care and responsiblity, improvement of environment through an assault on dereliction and use of better recreational and social activities. There is

[1] Some of these ideas are drawn from a discussion led by J. Bishop, University of Bristol at a Vandalism Seminar organized by the West Glamorgan Crime Prevention Panel, Port Talbot, 1980.

nothing new in this list but there can be little doubt that knowledge has often not led to action and scope for application of ideas of this kind is considerable.

One reaction against policy proposals of this kind which through more surveillance, community involvement or 'target-hardening' measures would reduce the vulnerability of specific areas or locations, is that the effect may be to displace crime rather than reduce it. Crime prevention policies and increased security programmes are sometimes criticized on the ground that although potential offenders will be deterred from such 'protected' places, they will merely transfer their activities to areas less able to afford such measures. The actual evidence on the question is limited but tends to suggest that physical crime prevention will at least deter less determined offenders who act largely on impulse. Press (1971) showed that increased police activity in one New York precinct shifted less crime to adjacent precincts than it prevented in the specific area. Hassell and Trethowan (1972) demonstrated a dramatic fall in Birmingham's suicide rate following the reduction in the toxic content of domestic gas; potential offenders did not actively search for other means. Home Office research into car security locks (P. Mayhew *et al.*, 1976) showed some displacement to older unprotected vehicles but also evidence of real reductions in offence rates. The implications of studies of this type of target-hardening procedures appear to be that some displacement effect will occur if there are other available 'targets' within relatively easy access and that crime prevention policies are anyway unlikely to deter the professional offender. It is also evident, however, that many offences are committed in a spontaneous way by individuals looking for general rather than specific outlets for their frustrations and for these crime preventive measures are likely to deter rather than displace:

> Criminal behaviour consists of a number of discrete activities which are heavily influenced by particular situational inducements and by the balance of risks and rewards involved. Upsetting this balance through measures which make it more difficult to act is unlikely to displace action to crime which serves different ends and for which different internal and external sanctions might apply (P. Mayhew *et al.*, 1976, p. 6).

Crime prevention in its various forms, from stronger locks to better surveillance and to community awareness is worth pursuing in order to reduce crime. A case can also be argued for rather more police emphasis on prevention rather than detection. It has to be recognized, however, that where specific schemes or a package of preventive measures are tried, it might not always be possible to demonstrate that they actually have the effect of reducing the crime rate. This is a necessary but again not a sufficient test of their success. It is at least as important to reduce the *fear* of crime which effects many thousands of urban dwellers. If applications of defensible space ideas and associated social policies can improve the quality of life in city neighbourhoods and increase feelings of well-being which people have in their everyday lives, then these are in themselves ample justifications for such policies. Most statistics show that the real chances of becoming a victim of crime, even in problem areas, are quite small. It is the fear, often exaggerated, of victimization which creates most of the stress and some alleviation of this would be a very positive contribution. The police actually witness and discover very few offences, citizen vigilante groups have disbanded out of the frustration of seeing nothing to report; crime prevention should focus on its passive role of allaying fear as well as on its active role as a deterrent to offenders.

RESEARCH DIRECTIONS

The last objective of this summary is that of identifying some of the directions in which research may develop. First it should be stated that a geography of crime must find its place within more general methodological developments in human geography (Herbert, 1980a). The idea of a conceptual framework which accommodates research at different levels of analysis (Fig. 2.1) has general applicability. Again, any 'geography' of crime cannot be divorced from criminological theory and its continually evolving ties with the philosophies of the social sciences. Strong parallelism in methodological debates within criminology and human geography are sources of strength which should be built on in constructive ways. As human geography evolves clearer involvement in interfaces with the social sciences rather than the natural sciences the methodological influence of the former will increase.

As it has so far emerged, the geography of crime has focused firmly on the local environment as a level of analysis. Awareness of other levels has grown but little substantive research has actually been accomplished. Hindess (1973), Sayer (1979) and others have given a clear lead on basic conceptual issues which need to be settled before official statistics on crime are used. National policies, extant laws, judicial practice and law enforcement are elements in the production of space which deserve study. In what has been termed the 'distribution' level, there are unresolved questions on levels of policing and their relationships to crime rates. This theme has several strands which need resolutions.

1. More policing leads to higher crime rates because as police 'burrow' into the dark area, more offences become known.
2. Police are especially active in known problem areas. Does this have the effect of ensuring that crime rates there remain high? This question is not well researched though Mawby (1979) argues that policing practice does not affect area crime rates.
3. Police are least well equipped to detect more sophisticated 'paper' crimes which involve professional and business classes.
4. Police hold discretionary powers: are these equitably applied over time and space?
5. Extra police resources need not bear a close relationship with official crime rates but can reduce fear and stress and improve the quality of life. This statement rests on the assumption that police have the confidence and respect of the public which, notwithstanding recent incidents in ethnic areas such as Bristol's St Pauls, is true for the vast majority of time.
6. Are there optimal location models which may improve the strategies of policing urban areas?

The police form one major component of the socio-legal system which produces spatial outcomes, another rests on the judiciary and ways in which its decisions are made. There is clearly a complexity of factors involved but preliminary evidence of the type described in Chapter 1 suggests there are differential outcomes which deserve closer research attention. Finally, at the 'distribution' level there are key issues surrounding the emergence of problem areas and the ways in which labels or reputations are established. The urban 'managers' figure prominently in this process and there is a shortage of good empirical research.

At the consumption level the actual record of research is most established. The priority here is to move out from traditional concerns with spatial pattern and association to encompass more aspects of the evolving social geographical perspective. Links between aggregate and individual scales of analysis remain to be developed, with area sampling frameworks there is scope for examining the spatial connotations of sociological theories such as that of subcultures. More behavioural research can both examine ways in which known offenders perceive the city and behave in space and how the general public react to the stress which crime generates. Some of Ley's (1974) early work on the effects of crime on other spatial behaviour provides guidelines here and the 'social dynamics' of place are critical components to be understood. The victims of crime are relatively understudied and as D. M. Smith (1974) argues, geographers could well divert some of their research attention to the question of 'who suffers where?'

Geographers are presented with many opportunities in the study of crime, both in its own right and as a facet of the more general social geography of the city. There is scope to develop the methodology of human geography, to illuminate spatial qualities, and to forge links with criminological theory and ongoing research in other disciplines. An ultimate objective of this work is to relate its findings to the practical needs of society and to the reform of both the local environments in which crime and criminals are found and of the conditions which produce them.

REFERENCES

Alihan, M. (1938) *Social Ecology*, Columbia University Press, New York.
Amir, M. (1971) *Patterns of Forcible Rape*, University of Chicago Press, Chicago.
Andry, R. (1960) *Delinquency and Parental Pathology*, Methuen, London, (rev. edn, 1971)
Bagot, J. H. (1971) *Juvenile Delinquency*, Cape, London.
Baldwin, J. (1974) 'Social area analysis and studies of delinquency', *Social Science Research* 3, 151–68.
Baldwin, J. (1975a) 'British area studies of crime: an assessment', *British Journal of Criminology* 15, 211–27.
Baldwin, J. (1975b) 'Urban criminality and the problem estate', *Local Government Studies*, 1, 12–20.
Baldwin, J. and **Bottoms, A. E.** (1976) *The Urban Criminal*, Tavistock, London.
Beccaria, C. B. (1953 edition) *An Essay on Crime and Punishment*, Academic Reprints, Stanford, California.
Bell, C. R. and **Newby, H.** (1978) 'Community, communion, class and community action: the social sources of the new urban politics', Ch. 8 pp. 283–301 in D. T. Herbert and R. J. Johnston, eds, *Social Areas in Cities*, Wiley, London.
Belson, W. A. (1975) *Juvenile Theft: the causal factors*, Harper and Row, London.
Berry, B. J. L. (1972) 'More on relevance and policy analysis', *Area* 4, 77–80.
Boggs, S. L. (1966) Urban crime patterns, *American Sociological Review* 30, 899–908.
Booth, C. (1891) *Life and Labour of the People*, Williams and Norgate, London.
Bottomley, A. K. and **Coleman, C. A.** (1976) 'Criminal statistics: the police role in the discovery and detection of crime', *International Journal of Crime and Punishment*, 4, 33–58.
Bottoms, A. E. (1974) Review, *British Journal of Criminology* 14, 203–6.
Bottoms, A. E. and **Xanthos, P.** (1979) *Housing policy and crime in the British public sector*, discussion paper, University of Sheffield.
Brantingham, P. J. and **P. L.** (1975) 'Residential burglary and urban form', *Urban Studies* 12, 273–84.
Brown, M. J. McCulloch, J. W., and **Hiscox, J.** (1972) 'Criminal offences in an urban area and their associated social variables', *British Journal of Criminology* 12, 250–68.
Burgess, E. W. (1925) 'The growth of the city', Ch. 2 pp. 47–62 in Park *et al.* (1925).
Burt, C. (1925) *The Young Delinquent*, London University Press, London.
Buttimer, A. (1976) 'Grasping the dynamism of life-world', *Annals of the Association of American Geographers*, 66, 277–92.
Caplow, T. (1949) 'The social ecology of Guatemala city', *Social Forces*, 28, 113–35.
Carr-Hill, R. A. and **Sterns, N. H.** (1979) *Crime, the Police and Criminal Statistics*, Academic Press, London.
Carter, R. L. (1974) 'The Criminal's Image of the City', unpublished doctoral thesis, University of Oklahoma, Norman.
Castle, I. M. and **Gittus. E.**, (1957) 'The distribution of social defects in Liverpool', *Sociological Review* 5, 43–64.
Chilton, R. J. (1964) 'Continuity in delinquency area research: a comparison of studies for Baltimore, Detroit and Indianapolis', *American Sociological Review* 29, 71–83.
Cicourel, A. V. (1968) *The Social Organisation of Juvenile Justice*, Wiley, New York.
Clarke, R. V. G., ed. (1978) *Tackling Vandalism*, Home Office Research Study, No. 47, HMSO, London.

Clinard M. B. (1962) 'The organization of U.C.D. services in the prevention of crime and juvenile delinquency', *International Review of Criminal Policy* **20**, 31–6.

Clinard M. B. (1978) *Cities without Crime: the case of Switzerland*, Cambridge University Press.

Cloward, R. A. and **Ohlin, L. E.** (1960) *Delinquency and Opportunity*, Free Press, Chicago.

Cohen, A. K. (1955) *Delinquent Boys*, Free Press, Chicago.

Corsi, T. M. and **Harvey, M. E.** (1975) 'The socio-economic determinants of crime in the city of Cleveland', *Tijdschrift voor Economische – Sociale Geografie*, **66**, 323–36.

Cox, K. (1973) *Conflict, Power and Politics in the City: a geographic view*, McGraw-Hill, New York.

Damer, S. (1974) 'Wine Alley: the sociology of a dreadful enclosure', *Sociological Review* **22**, 221–48.

De Fleur, L. B. (1967) 'Ecological variables in the cross-cultural study of delinquency', *Social Forces*, **45**, 556–70.

Denning, R. (1973) 'Growing up in Ely' Vol. 7, 149–56, in S. Williams, ed., *The Cardiff Book*, Williams, Cowbridge.

Downes, D. M. (1966) *The Delinquent Solution*, Routledge and Kegan Paul, London.

Durkheim, E. (1966 edition) *Suicide: a study in sociology*, Free Press, Chicago.

Edwards, A. (1973) 'Sex and area variations in delinquency in an English city', *British Journal of Criminology*, **13**, 121–37.

Eisenstad, S. N. and **Curelaru, M.** (1976) *The Form of Sociology: paradigms and crises*, Wiley, London.

Elmhorn, K. (1965) 'Study in self-reported delinquency among school-children', *Scandinavian Studies in Criminology*, **1**, 117–46.

Evans, D. J. (1973) 'A comparative study of urban social structures in South Wales', **Chap. 5**, pp. 87–101 in Institute British Geographers. *Special Publication, 5*, Social Patterns in Cities.

Evans, D. J. (1978) 'Urban structures and social problems', unpublished Ph.D. thesis, University of Wales.

Eyles, J. D. (1979) 'Area-based policies for the inner city: context, problems and prospects', **Ch. 12** pp. 226–43 in Herbert and Smith (1979).

Fletcher, J. (1849) 'Moral statistics of England and Wales', *Journal of the Royal Statistical Society of London*, **12**, 151–81, 189–335.

Forman, R. E. (1963) 'Delinquency rates and opportunities for subcultural transmission', *Journal of Criminal Law, Criminology and Police Science* **54**, 317–21.

Gill, O. (1977) *Luke Street*, Macmillan, London.

Gittus, E. and **Stephens, C. J.** (1973) 'Some Problems in the Use of Canonical Analysis', discussion paper, Newcastle University.

Glaser, B. G. and **Strauss, A. L.** (1968) *The Discovery of Grounded Theory: strategies for qualitative research*, Weidenfeld and Nicolson, London.

Glueck, S. and **Glueck, E.** (1950) *Unravelling Juvenile Delinquency*, Commonwealth Fund, New York.

Glueck, S. and **E. Glueck,** (1952) *Delinquency in the Making*, Harper, New York.

Gold, M. E. (1966) 'Undetected delinquent behaviour', *Journal of Research in Crime and Delinquency*, **3**, 27–46.

Gordon, R. A. (1967) 'Issues in the ecological study of delinquency', *American Sociological Review*, **32**, 927–44.

Guerry, A. M. (1833) *Essai sur la Statistique Morale de la France avec Cartes*, Crochard, Paris.

Hargreaves, D. (1967) *Social Relations in a Secondary School*, Routledge and Kegan Paul, London.

Haring, L. L., ed. (1972) *Summary Report of Spatial Studies of Juvenile Delinquency in Phoenix, Arizona*, Geography Dept., Arizona State University.

Harries, K. D. (1974) *The Geography of Crime and Justice*, McGraw-Hill, New York.

Harries, K. D. (1980) *Crime and the Environment*, Charles C. Thomas, Springfield, Illinois.

Harries, K. D. and **Brunn, S. D.** (1978) *The Geography of Laws and Justice*, Praeger, New York.

Hassel, C. and **Trethowan, W. H.** (1972) 'Suicide in Birmingham', *British Medical Journal* **1**, 717–18.

Hauser, D. P. (1975) 'Some problems in the use of stepwise regression techniques in geographical research', *Canadian Geographer* **19**, 148–58.

Hawkins, R. (1973) 'Who called the cops? Decisions to report criminal victimizations', *Law and Society Review*, **7**, 427–44.

Hay, A. M. (1979) 'Positivism in human geography: reply to critics, **Ch. 1**, 1–26 in Herbert and Johnston (1979) Vol. 2.

Hayner, N. S. (1946) 'Criminogenic zones in Mexico City', *American Sociological Review*, **11**, 428–38.

Haynes, R. M. (1973) 'Crime rates and city-size in America', *Area*, **5**, 162–5.
Herbert, D. T. (1970) 'Principal components analysis and urban-social structure: a study of Cardiff and Swansea', in H. Carter and W. K. D. Davis (eds) *Urban Essays: studies in the geography of Wales*, Longman, London, Ch. 5, pp. 79–100.
Herbert, D. T. (1973) *Residential Mobility and Preference: a study of Swansea*, Institute British Geographers Special Publication, No. 5, Social Patterns in Cities, 179–94.
Herbert, D. T. (1975) 'Urban deprivation: definition, measurement, and spatial qualities,' *Geographical Journal*, **141**, 362–72.
Herbert, D. T. (1976) 'The study of delinquency areas: a social geographical approach', *Transactions of the Institute British Geographers*, new series, **1**, 472–92.
Herbert, D. T. (1977a) 'An areal and ecological analysis of delinquency residence: Cardiff 1966 and 1971', *Tijdschrift voor Economische en Sociale Geografie*, **68**, 83–99.
Herbert, D. T. (1977b) 'Crime, delinquency and the urban environment', *Progress in Human Geography* **1**, 208–39.
Herbert, D. T. (1979a) 'Geographical perspectives and urban problems', Ch. 1, p. 1–10, in Herbert and Smith (1979).
Herbert, D.T. (1979b) 'Urban crime: a geographical perspective', Ch. 7, pp. 117–38, in Ibid.
Herbert, D. T. (1980a) *The Social Geography of the City*, Social Science Research Council report, University College of Swansea.
Herbert, D.T. (1980b) 'Geography and urban studies: the spatial dimension', *Sociol. Review Monograph*, Keele.
Herbert, D. T. and **Evans, D. J.** (1974) 'Urban sub-areas as sampling frameworks for social survey', *Town Planning Review* **45**, 171–88.
Herbert, D. T. and **Johnston, R. J.** eds (1978) *Geography and the Urban Environment*, Wiley, London, Vol. 1.
Herbert, D.T. and **Smith, D. M.**, eds (1979) *Social Problems and the City: geographical perspectives*, Oxford University Press.
Hillier, B. (1973) 'In defence of space', *Royal Institute of British Architects Journal* Nov., 539–44.
Hindess, B. (1973) *The Use of Official Statistics in Sociology*, Macmillan, London.
Hirschi, T. and **Selvin, H. C.** (1967) *Delinquency Research: an appraisal of analytic methods*, Macmillan, London.
Hood, R. and **Sparks, R.** (1970) *Key Issues in Criminology*, Weidenfeld and Nicolson, London.
Jacobs, J. (1961) *Death and Life of Great American Cities*, Random House, New York.
Jephcott, P. and **Carter, M. P.** (1954) 'The Social Background of Delinquency', discussion report, University of Nottingham.
Johnstone, J. W. C. (1978) 'Social class, social areas and delinquency', *Sociology and Social Research*, **63**, 49–72.
Jones, C. D. (1934) *Social Survey of Merseyside*, Liverpool University Press,
Kitsuse, J. I. and **Cicourel, A. K.** (1963) 'A note on the use of official statistics', *Social Problems*, **11**, 131–9.
Klare, H. J. (1966) *Changing Concepts of Crime and its Treatment*, Pergamon, Oxford.
Knox, P. L. (1975) *Social Well-being: a spatial perspective*, Oxford University Press,
Kobrin, S. (1951) The conflict of values in delinquency areas, *American Sociological Review*, **16**, 653–61.
Lambert, J. R. (1970) *Crime, Police and Race Relations*, Oxford University Press,
Lander, B. (1954) *Towards an Understanding of Juvenile Delinquency*, Columbia University Press, New York.
Leather, A. and **Matthews, A.** (1973) 'What the architect can do', Ch. 8, pp. 117–72 in C. Ward (ed.) *Vandalism*, Architectural Press, London.
Lee, R. (1979) 'The economic bases of social problems in the city', Ch. 4, pp. 47–62 in Herbert and Smith (1979).
Lee, Y., and **Egan, F. J.** (1972) 'The geography of urban crime: the spatial pattern of serious crime in the city of Denver', *Proceedings of the Association of American Geographers*, **4**, 59–64.
Lemon, N. (1974) 'Training, personality, and attitude as determinants of Magistrates' sentencing' *British Journal of Criminology*, **14**, 34–48.
Ley, D. (1974) *The Black Inner City as Frontier Outpost*, Association of American Geographers, Washington.
Ley, D. (1975) 'The street gang in its milieu', in H. Rose and G. Gappert (eds) *The Social Economy of Cities*, Sage, New York, Ch. 7, pp. 247–73.
Ley, D. (1977) 'Social geography and the taken-for-granted world', *Transactions of the Institute of British Geographers*, new series, **2**, 498–512.

Ley, D. and **Cybriwsky, R.** (1974a) 'The spatial ecology of stripped cars', *Environment and Behaviour*, **6**, 53–67.

Ley, D. and **Cybriwsky** (1974b) 'Urban graffiti as territorial markers', *Annals of the Association of American Geographers*, **64**, 491–505.

Lombroso, C. (1874) *Crime, its Causes and Remedies*, Patterson, Smith, Montclair, New Jersey.

Lottier, S. (1938) 'Distribution of criminal offences in sectional regions', *Journal of Criminal Law Criminology and Police Science*, **29**, 329–44.

Mack, J. (1964) 'Full-time miscreants, delinquent neighbourhoods and criminal networks', *British Journal of Sociology*, **15**, 38–53.

McClintock, F. H., **Avison, N. H.**, **Savill, N. C.** and **Worthington, V. I.** (1963) *Crimes of Violence*, Macmillan, London.

McClintock, F. H. and **Avison, N. H.** (1968) *Crime in England and Wales*, Heinemann, London.

Mangin, W. (1962) 'Mental health and migration to cities: a Peruvian case', Ch. 5, pp. 313–20, in P., Meadows and E. H. Mizruchi (eds) *Urbanism, Urbanisation and Change: comparative perspectives*, Addison Wesley, Reading, Mass.

Mannheim, H. (1965) *Comparative Criminology*, Routledge and Kegan Paul, London.

Matza, D. (1964) *Delinquency and Drift*, Wiley, New York.

Matza, D. (1969) *Becoming Deviant*, Prentice-Hall, Englewood Cliffs.

Mawby, R. I. (1977a) 'Defensible space: a theoretical and empirical approach', *Urban Studies*, **14**, 169–79.

Mawby, R. I. (1977b) 'Kiosk vandalism: a Sheffield study', *British Journal of Criminology*, **17**, 30–46.

Mawby, R. I. (1979) 'Policing residential areas of the city', discussion paper, University of Sheffield.

Mayhew, H. (1862) *London Labour and the London Poor*, Griffin-Bohn, London.

Mayhew, P. (1979) 'Defensible space: the current status of a crime prevention theory', *Howard Journal*, **18**, 150–9.

Mayhew, P., **Clarke, R. V. G.**, **Sturman, A.** and **Hough, J. M.** (1976) *Crime as Opportunity*, Home Office Research Unit, Study No. 34, HMSO, London.

Mayhew, P. *et al.* (1979) *Crime in Public View*, Home Office Research Unit, Study No. 49, HMSO, London.

Mays, J. B. (1963) 'Delinquency areas: a re-assessment', *British Journal of Criminology*, **3**, 216–30.

Merton, R. K. (1938) 'Social structure and anomie', *American Sociological Review*, **3**, 672–82.

Michelson, W. (1970) *Man and his Urban Environment*, Addison-Wesley, Reading, Mass.

Miller, W. B. (1958) 'Lower-class culture as a generating milieu of gang delinquency', *Journal of Social Issues*, **14**, 5–19.

Morris, T. P. (1957) *The Criminal Area: a study in social ecology*, Routledge and Kegan Paul, London.

Murray, R. and **Boal, F. W.** (1979) 'The social ecology of urban violence', Ch. 8, pp. 139–57, in Herbert and Smith (1979).

Nader, R. and **Green, M.** (1972) *Crime in the Suites*, New Republic, 17–21.

National Criminal Justice Information and Statistical Service (1977) *Criminal Victimization in the United States*, Springfield, Virgina.

Nettler, G. (1974) *Explaining Crime*, McGraw-Hill, New York.

Newman, O. (1972) *Defensible Space*, Macmillan, New York.

Newman, O. (1976) *Design Guidelines for Creating Defensible Space*, US Dept. of Justice, Washington.

Pablant, P. and **Baxter, J. C.** (1975) 'Environmental correlates of school vandalism', *Journal of the American Institute of Planners*, **41**, 270–9.

Pahl, R. E. (1979) 'Socio-political factors in resource allocation', Chapter 3 pp. 33–46 in Herbert and Smith (1979).

Park, R. E., **Burgess, E. W.** and **Mackenzie, R. D.** (1925) *The City*, University of Chicago Press, Chicago.

Peet, R. (1975) 'The geography of crime: a political critique', *Professional Geographer*, **27**, 277–80.

Peet, R. (1976) 'Further comment on the geography of crime', *Professional Geographer* **28**, 96–100.

Peet, R. ed. (1977) *Radical Geography*, Methuen, London.

Phillips P. D. (1972) 'A prologue to the geography of crime', *Proceedings of the Association of American Geographers* **4**, 59–64.

Phillipson, M. (1971) *Sociological Aspects of Crime and Delinquency*, Routledge and Kegan Paul, London.

Polk, K. (1957) 'Juvenile delinquency and social areas', *Social Problems*, **5**, 214–17.

Polk, K. (1967) 'Urban social areas and delinquency', *Social Problems*, **14**, 320–5.

Press, S. J. (1971) *Some Effects of an Increase in Police Manpower in the 20th Precinct of New York City*, Rand, New York.

Pyle G. F., ed. (1974) *The Spatial Dynamics of Crime*, Geography Research Paper 159, University of Chicago.

Radford, J. (1979) 'Testing the model of the pre-industrial city: the case of ante-bellum Charleston, S. Carolina', *Transactions Institute of British Geographers*, **4**, 392–410.

Repetto, T. A. (1974) *Residential Crime*, Ballinger, Cambridge, Mass.

Rex, J. and **Moore, R.** (1967) *Race, Community and Conflict*, Oxford University Press,

Rock, P. (1979) 'Another commonsense conception of deviancy', *Sociology*, **13**, 75–88.

Rushton, G. (1979) *Optimal Location of Facilities*, Compress Inc., Hanover, New Hampshire.

Russell, C. (1973) 'The formation of stereotypes by the police', unpublished MA thesis, Sussex University.

Rutter, M. and **Madge, N.** (1976) *Cycles of Disadvantage*, Heinemann, London,

Sainsbury, P. (1955) *Suicide in London: an ecological study*, Chapman and Hall, London.

Saunders, P. (1980) *Urban Politics: a sociological interpretation*, Penguin, Harmondsworth.

Sayer, R. A. (1979) 'Epistemology and concepts of people and nature in geography', *Geoforum*, **10**, 19–44.

Scarr, H. A. (1972) *Patterns of Burglary*, US Dept. of Justice, Washington.

Schmid, C. F. (1960) 'Urban crime areas', *American Sociological Review*, **25**, 527–54 and 655–78.

Scott, P. (1965) Delinquency, mobility, and broken homes in Horbart', *Australian Journal of Social Issues*, **2**, 10–22.

Scott, P. (1972) 'The spatial analysis of crime and delinquency', *Australian Geographical Studies*, **10**, 1–18.

Sellin, T. (1937) 'Crime in the recession', *Social Science Research Council, Bulletin* **27**, New York.

Sennett, R. (1973) *The Uses of Disorder*, Penguin, Harmondsworth.

Shannon, L. W. (1954) 'The spatial distribution of criminal offences by states', *Journal of Criminal Law, Criminology and Police Science*, **45**, 264–73.

Shaw, C. R. (1930) *The Jack-roller*, University of Chicago Press, Chicago.

Shaw, C. R. and **McKay, H. D.** (1942) *Juvenile Delinquency and Urban Areas*, University of Chicago Press, Chicago, rev. edn, 1969.

Sheldon, W. H. (1949) *The Varieties of Delinquent Youth*, Harper, New York.

Smith, C. J. (1980) 'Neighbourhood effects on mental health', Ch. 10, pp. 363–415, in Herbert and Johnston (1980), Vol. 3.

Smith, D. M. (1974) *Crime Rates as Territorial Social Indicators*, Queen Mary College, London, Occasional Papers in Geography, No. 1.

Snodgrass, J. (1976) 'Clifford R. Shaw and Henry D. McKay: Chicago criminologists', *British Journal of Criminology*, **16**, 1–19.

South Wales Echo (1975) Thomson Press, Cardiff.

Sprott, W. J. H. (1972) 'Delinquency areas: Nottingham', Ch. 4, pp. 30–44 in J. B. Mays, (ed.) *Juvenile Delinquency, the Family, and the Social Group*, Longman, London.

Stedman-Jones, G. (1971) *Outcast London: a study in the relationships between classes in Victorian society*, Oxford University Press.

Strange, K. (1980) 'In search of the celestial empire: crime in Merthyr, 1830–60', *Llafur*, **3**, 44–86.

Sutherland, E. H. (1940) 'White collar criminality', *American Sociological Review*, **5**, 1–12.

Sutherland, E. H. and **Cressey, D. R.** (1970) *Principles of Criminology*, Lippincott, Philadelphia.

Suttles, G. (1968) *The Social Order of the Slum*, University of Chicago Press, Chicago.

Suttles, G. (1975) 'Community design: the search for participation in metropolitan society', Ch. 6. pp. 235–98 in A. H. Hawley and V. P. Rock (eds) *Metropolitan America in Contemporary Perspective*, Sage, New York.

Tarling, R. (1979) *Sentencing Practice in Magistrates' Courts*, Home Office Research Unit, Study No. 56, HMSO, London.

Taylor, I., Walton, P., and **Young, J.** (1973) *The New Criminology*, Routledge and Kegan Paul, London.

Taylor, L. (1973) 'The meaning of environment', Ch. 2, pp. 54–63 in C. Ward (ed.) *Vandalism*, Architectural Press, London.

Thrasher, C. (1927) *The Gang*, University of Chicago Press, Chicago.

Timms, D. W. G. (1965) 'The spatial distribution of social deviants in Luton, England', *Australia New Zealand Journal of Sociology*, **1**, 38–52.

Tobias, J. J. (1967) *Crime and Industrial Society in the Nineteenth Century*, Harmondsworth, Penguin.

Tobias, J. J. (1976) 'A statistical study of a nineteenth century criminal area', *British Journal of Criminology*, **14**, 221–35.

Trasler, G. (1963) 'Theoretical problems in the explanation of delinquent behaviour', *Education Research*, **6**, 42–9.

Waller, I. and **Okihiro, N.** (1978) *Burglary: the victim and the public*, University of Toronto Press, Toronto.

Wallis, C. P. and **Maliphant, R.** (1967) 'Delinquent areas in the county of London', *British Journal of Criminology*, **7**, 250–84.

West, D. J. (1967) *The Young Offender*, Duckworth, London.

West, D. J. and **Farringdon, D. P.** (1973) *Who Becomes Delinquent?* Heinemann, London.

Wheeler, S. (1976) 'Trends and patterns in the sociological study of crime', *Social Problems*, **23**, 525–34.

Wiles, P. ed. (1976) *The Sociology of Crime and Delinquency in Britain*, Martin Robertson, London.

Willie, C. V. (1967) 'The relative contribution of family status and economic status to juvenile delinquency', *Social Problems*, **14**, 326–35.

Wilson, R. (1963) *Difficult Housing Estates*, Tavistock, London.

Wilson, S. (1978) 'Vandalism and defensible space on London housing estates', Ch. 4, pp. 41–65, in Clarke (1978).

Winchester, S. W. (1978) 'Two suggestions for developing the geographical study of crime', *Area*, **10**, 116–20.

Wood, E (1961) *Housing Design: a social theory*, Citizens' Housing and Planning Council, New York.

Wootton, B. (1959) *Social Science and Social Pathology*, Allen and Unwin, London.

INDEX